Rustic Fruit Desserts

Rustic Fruit Desserts

DELICIOUSLY COMFORTING RECIPES
FROM COBBLERS TO PIES

RYLAND PETERS & SMALL
LONDON • NEW YORK

Senior Designer Toni Kay
Commissioning Editor Alice Sambrook
Production Controller Mai-Ling Collyer
Art Director Leslie Harrington
Editorial Director Julia Charles
Publisher Cindy Richards
Indexer Vanessa Bird

First published in 2018 by
Ryland Peters & Small
20–21 Jockey's Fields, London WC1R 4BW
and
341 E 116th St, New York NY 10029
www.rylandpeters.com

10 9 8 7 6 5 4 3 2 1

Recipe collection compiled by
Alice Sambrook

Text copyright © Carol Hilker, Dunja
Gulin, Hannah Miles, Janet Sawyer,
Jenna Zoe, Jordan Bourke, Kiki Bee,
Laura Washburn, Leah Vanderveldt,
Lizzie Kamenetzky, Maxine Clark,
Julian Day, Rosa Rigby, Ross Dobson,
Sarah Randall, Suzy Pelta, Tori Haschka,
Will Torrent, Valerie Aikman-Smith and
Victoria Glass.

Design and photographs copyright
© Ryland Peters & Small 2018

ISBN: 978-1-78879-033-8

Printed in China

The authors' moral rights have
been asserted. All rights reserved.
No part of this publication may be
reproduced, stored in a retrieval
system or transmitted in any form or
by any means, electronic, mechanical,
photocopying or otherwise, without
the prior permission of the publisher.

A CIP record for this book is available
from the British Library.

US Library of Congress Cataloging-in-
Publication Data has been applied for.

NOTES:
• Both British (Metric) and American
(Imperial plus US cups) measurements
are included in these recipes for your
convenience, however it is important
to work with one set of measurements
and not alternate between the two
within a recipe.
• All spoon measurements are level
unless otherwise specified.
• All eggs are medium (UK) or large (US),
unless specified as large, in which case
US extra-large should be used. Uncooked
eggs should not be served to the very
old, frail, young children, pregnant
women or those with compromised
immune systems.
• Ovens should be preheated to the
specified temperatures. We recommend
using an oven thermometer. If using a
fan-assisted oven, adjust temperatures
according to the manufacturer's
instructions.
• When a recipe calls for the grated
zest of citrus fruit, buy unwaxed fruit
and wash well before using. If you can
only find treated fruit, scrub well in
warm soapy water before using.

Contents

Introduction

Comforting, homely and warming, a rustic fruit dessert is the edible equivalent of a hug in the softest blanket at the end of a long day. Just a spoonful of one of these treats, drowned in the cream, custard or ice cream of your choice is enough to melt troubles away.

Whether you are looking for a quick midweek fix or a dish for easy weekend entertaining, you'll find the perfect recipe here. Choose from the myriad fresh fruits included in these pages, from apples, pears and rhubarb to berries, peaches and plums, to tropical pineapple and mango, take your cue from the season and make the most of these fresh ingredients.

Try a classic British crumble or American-style crisp or cobbler – these have a stewed fruit base and a topping that looks better scattered or dropped on at random – the more rustic-looking the better!

Everyone appreciates a slice of a fine fruit pie or tart, with buttery pastry and unctuous, sweet filling – here you can learn how to make all the classics. Pastry recipes are included, but feel free to use ready-made if short on time.

There are plenty of long-cherished recipes waiting to be re-discovered. You could opt for the fabulous French clafoutis, which comprises of fresh fruit baked inside a light, sweet batter, or a satisfying slump, which is just about as easy and filling as the name suggests.

For after dinner, try a rustic fruit pudding such as the bread and butter or croissant bake; these use up leftovers from the breakfast table, and can be made to look much more elegant than you might expect. Finally, let yourself be tempted by a gorgeously moist dessert cake, ideal with afternoon tea.

These straightforward recipes are a cinch to put together, leaving you free to relax as the fruit bubbles away and the topping turns golden, filling your kitchen with delicious aromas. With this book by your side you'll never be lost for a quick, easy and comforting dessert recipe again.

Crumbles, crisps and cobblers

Apple and blackberry crumble

6 Braeburn apples
(or another similarly sharp
and sweet variety)

freshly squeezed juice
of ½ lemon

350 g/12 oz. fresh blackberries

1 tablespoon caster/
granulated sugar

CRUMBLE TOPPING

100 g/¾ cup plain/
all-purpose flour

50 g/½ cup ground almonds

50 g½ cup coarse pinhead/
large steel-cut oats

pinch of salt

seeds of 1 vanilla pod/bean

100 g/1 stick minus 1
tablespoon cold unsalted
butter, cubed

hot custard or chilled cream,
to serve

medium ovenproof dish

SERVES 8–10

Crumble, one of the UK's favourite winter puddings, is a delicious result of World War II's food rationing. Butter, eggs and sugar were all in short supply, which resulted in pies and sponge cakes being replaced by the more humble yet still delicious crumble. Here, the traditional topping is jazzed up to include nuts and oats, with a classic apple and blackberry filling.

Preheat the oven to 180°C (350°F) Gas 4.

Core and slice the apples. You can peel them if you prefer, or leave the skin on for a rustic effect. Toss the apples slices in the lemon juice and put them in the ovenproof dish. Scatter the blackberries on top and sprinkle over the sugar.

Put the flour, almonds, oats, salt and vanilla in a large bowl and mix together until well combined. Add the butter and rub into the mixture with your fingers until it resembles coarse breadcrumbs. Tip the crumble topping over the fruit, but do not be tempted to press it down.

Bake in the preheated oven for 35–40 minutes, or until the top is golden and the fruit is soft and bubbling. Leave the crumble to cool for 15–20 minutes before serving warm with lashings of hot custard or chilled cream, as preferred.

Rhubarb crumble

Unlike most other seasonal fruits, 'forced' out-of-season rhubarb is actually better for cooking, with a less fibrous texture than the naturally grown variety, and a delicate sour flavour. Serve this crumble with a sweet ice cream to perfectly complement the natural tartness of the fruit.

800 g/1¾ lb. forced rhubarb, trimmed

210 g/1 cup coconut palm sugar

zest of 1 lemon, peeled off in large strips

1 teaspoon pure vanilla extract

CRUMBLE TOPPING

2½ tablespoons sunflower spread

2 tablespoons coconut butter

80 g/⅔ cup white spelt flour

70 g/⅔ cup rolled/ old fashioned oats

50 g/⅓ cup whole almonds, lightly crushed

pinch of sea salt

ice cream, to serve (optional)

medium ovenproof dish

SERVES 6–8

Preheat the oven to 200°C (400°F) Gas 6.

Cut the rhubarb into 5 cm/2 inch chunks. Place a large, heavy-based saucepan over a medium heat. Add the rhubarb, 150 g/¾ cup of the sugar (or add up to 50 g/¼ cup extra if you prefer a sweeter taste), the lemon zest strips and vanilla. Cook over a low heat for about 15 minutes until the rhubarb is tender and the sugar has become syrup. Remove from the heat and set aside.

In a large bowl, rub the sunflower spread and coconut butter into the flour with your fingers until it resembles coarse breadcrumbs. Mix in the oats, remaining sugar, almonds and salt. Place the rhubarb in the ovenproof dish, remove the lemon zest strips, and top with the crumble without pressing down.

Bake in the preheated oven for about 25 minutes until the topping is golden brown. Leave to cool for 5 minutes, then serve with a scoop of ice cream, if liked.

Peach crumble

1.8 kg/about 8 firm but
  ripe peaches

2–3 tablespoons apple juice
  concentrate

1 tablespoon plain/
  all-purpose flour

pinch of salt

CRUMBLE TOPPING

80 g/^{2}/$_3$ cup hazelnuts

65 g/^{1}/$_2$ cup plain/
  all-purpose flour

50 g/^{1}/$_2$ cup rolled/old
  fashioned oats

grated zest of 1 orange

^{1}/$_4$ teaspoon ground cinnamon

^{1}/$_8$ teaspoon bourbon
  vanilla powder

pinch of salt

85 g/^{1}/$_3$ cup brown rice
  or agave syrup

50 g/^{1}/$_3$ cup margarine,
  at room temperature

custard, to serve (optional)

medium ovenproof dish

SERVES 6–8

Juicy, fragrant peaches make a luxurious, summery dessert. It's especially nice to serve this crumble after dinner on a summer's evening when the temperature outside drops and you need some extra warming up from the inside.

Preheat the oven to 150°C (300°F) Gas 2.

First, put the hazelnuts for the crumble topping in a baking pan and roast in the preheated oven for 8–10 minutes. Rub off any skins that have loosened, then roughly chop by hand or in a food processor. Big pieces will burn while the crumble is baking, so make them quite small. Put the flour, oats, orange zest, cinnamon, vanilla powder and salt in a bowl and stir. Add the syrup and mix well, then rub the margarine into the mixture with your fingers until it resembles coarse breadcrumbs. Stir in the chopped nuts and set aside.

Preheat the oven to 180°C (350°F) Gas 4.

Blanch the peaches in a saucepan of boiling water for 1–2 minutes – just long enough to be able to peel the skins off easily. Transfer to a bowl of cold water so you don't burn your fingers, then peel off the skins. Halve and pit the peaches and cut them into wedges. Toss them with the apple juice concentrate, flour and salt. Spread the peach wedges out in the ovenproof dish and cover them evenly with the crumble, without pressing the mixture down.

Bake in the preheated oven for about 35 minutes or until the crumble topping is golden brown and the juice is bubbling up around the edges. Serve warm with custard, if you like.

Pear, apple and pecan crumble

2 cooking apples
(such as Lord Derby,
Bramley, Pippin or Winesap)

2 pears

80 g/scant 1/2 cup coconut
palm sugar (or more to taste)

freshly squeezed juice of
1/2 lemon

60 g/1/2 cup pecans,
lightly roasted

CRUMBLE TOPPING

30 g/2 tablespoons sunflower
spread

30 g/2 tablespoons coconut oil

70 g/1/2 cup plus
1 tablespoon rice flour

70 g/2/3 cup rolled/
old fashioned oats

60 g/1/3 cup coconut palm
sugar

2 tablespoons maple syrup

1 teaspoon ground cinnamon

frozen coconut yogurt, to serve
(optional)

medium ovenproof dish

SERVES 6–8

Apple crumble is all about warmth, familiarity and that comforting smell of a freshly baked dessert. This version is spruced with the addition of pears and pecans, which add an extra dimension of flavour and texture. You may not even notice that this healthy crumble is made without dairy and refined sugar.

To make the filling, peel and core the apples and pears. Cut into large chunks and place in a large saucepan mixed together with the coconut sugar, lemon juice and 1 tablespoon of water. Stew over low–medium heat until half-cooked. Taste and add more sugar, if necessary. Transfer to the ovenproof dish with all the juices and mix in the pecans (reserving some for the top). Allow to cool while you make the topping.

Preheat the oven to 180°C (350°F) Gas 4.

To make the topping, in a large bowl, rub the sunflower spread and coconut oil into the flour with your fingers until it resembles fine breadcrumbs. Add the oats, sugar, maple syrup and cinnamon and mix thoroughly. Sprinkle the topping over the filling.

Bake the crumble in the preheated oven for about 35–45 minutes or until the fruit is tender and the juices are bubbling and the topping is golden. Sprinkle the remaining pecans over the top and serve with frozen coconut yogurt, if you like.

Plum and amaretto crumble

This is the ultimate comfort food. Here, tangy booze-infused plums with a hint of almond and vanilla, are buried beneath a buttery, melt-in-the-mouth crumble – what could be better!

800 g/1¾ lb. ripe red plums, halved and pitted

1 vanilla pod/bean

85 g/⅓ cup plus 2 tablespoons caster/granulated sugar

100 ml/⅓ cup Amaretto, or other almond-flavoured liqueur

CRUMBLE TOPPING

115 g/generous 1 cup ground almonds

115 g/1 stick cold unsalted butter, cubed

115 g/1¼ cups rolled/old fashioned oats

60 g/⅓ cup caster/granulated sugar

cream, to serve (optional)

large ovenproof dish, buttered

SERVES 8

Preheat the oven to 180°C (350°F) Gas 4.

Put the plums in a large saucepan. Split the vanilla pod/bean in half with a sharp knife and use the tip of the knife to scrape the seeds directly into the saucepan. Add the vanilla pod/bean, sugar and Amaretto. Simmer the plums over a gentle heat for about 5 minutes, until softened. Remove and discard the vanilla pod/bean and transfer the fruit to the prepared baking dish.

To make the crumble topping, put the ground almonds in a mixing bowl and rub in the butter with your fingers until the mixture resembles coarse breadcrumbs. Stir in the oats and sugar. Sprinkle the mixture over the plums and bake in the preheated oven for 35–40 minutes, until the topping is golden brown and the plum juices are bubbling around the edge of the dish. Serve warm with cream, if you like.

Chocolate and berry crumble

500 g/18 oz. mixed berries
(raspberries, blackberries,
blueberries, etc.)

1 tablespoon caster/
granulated sugar

seeds of 1 vanilla pod/bean

CRUMBLE TOPPING

200 g/1½ cups plain/
all-purpose flour

25 g/3½ tablespoons
cocoa powder

pinch of salt

100 g/1 stick minus 1
tablespoon cold unsalted
butter, cubed

100 g/½ cup caster/
granulated sugar

custard, to serve (optional)

large ovenproof dish

SERVES 8–10

A failsafe crumble filling with the addition of a quirky cocoa topping, you could even add a small splash of Kirsch to the fruit for an extra touch of decadence, if you like. This dessert is especially delicious served with vanilla custard.

Put the berries in the ovenproof dish. Sprinkle over the sugar, add the vanilla seeds and mix everything together until the fruit is evenly coated. Set aside.

For the crumble, sift the flour, cocoa and salt together into a large bowl and mix until well combined. Add the butter and rub the mixture lightly with your fingers until it resembles coarse breadcrumbs. Stir through the sugar and tip the crumble over the fruit, but do not press it down.

Bake in the preheated oven for 35–40 minutes, or until the top is golden brown and the fruit is soft and bubbling. Leave the crumble to cool for 15–20 minutes before serving with lashings of hot custard, if liked.

Chocolate, pear and winter spice crumble

RED WINE GANACHE

125 g/1 cup dark/bittersweet chocolate, finely chopped

90 ml/¹⁄₃ cup red wine

PEAR FILLING

6 pears, peeled, cored and chopped

75 ml/scant ¹⁄₃ cup red wine

25 ml/2 tablespoons ruby port

75 g/¹⁄₄ cup honey

1 star anise

1 cinnamon stick

150 g/1¹⁄₂ cups blackberries

CRUMBLE TOPPING

110 g/³⁄₄ cup blanched hazelnuts

75 g/generous ¹⁄₂ cup plain/all-purpose flour

1 tablespoon cocoa powder

50 g/¹⁄₄ cup soft light brown sugar

75 g/³⁄₄ stick cold unsalted butter, cubed

1 teaspoon ground cinnamon

1 teaspoon mixed spice/apple pie spice

pinch of salt

medium ovenproof dish

SERVES 8

This warming winter dessert is something special, with pears poached in spiced red wine and a nutty chocolate crumble topping. Perfect for chocolate lovers, the red wine ganache tastes almost like mulled wine chocolate sauce, making it ideal for serving over the festive season.

To make the ganache, put the chopped chocolate into a heatproof bowl and set aside. Heat the red wine in a small saucepan set over a medium heat to just below boiling. Add the chocolate and stir until smooth. Leave to cool, then cover and refrigerate until firm.

For the pear filling, put the pears in a saucepan with the red wine, port and honey. Add the star anise and cinnamon stick, then set the pan over a medium heat and cook for about 10 minutes, until the pears start to soften. Stir in the blackberries and transfer to the ovenproof dish. Remove the star anise and cinnamon and set aside.

Preheat the oven to 180°C (350°F) Gas 4.

To make the crumble, tip 40 g/¹⁄₄ cup of the blanched hazelnuts into a food processor and blitz until roughly chopped. Transfer to a large bowl and set aside. Tip the remaining hazelnuts into the food processor and pulse until finely ground. Add the flour, cocoa powder, sugar, diced butter, spices and salt and pulse again until the butter has been rubbed into the dry ingredients and the mixture starts to clump together. Transfer to the bowl with the chopped hazelnuts and mix. Transfer the crumble mixture to a baking sheet in an even layer and bake in the preheated oven for 20 minutes until it starts to crisp.

To assemble, place teaspoons of the red wine ganache around the pears and blackberries in the baking dish. Top with the pre-baked crumble and bake in the oven for a further 20 minutes until the fruit is bubbling and the topping is crisp. Remove from the oven and serve immediately.

Banana and Irish cream crumbles

These little guys are the perfect 'Quick, I'm hosting a dinner party and need a fabulous humdinger of a dessert!' dish. That and, of course, they are one of your five a day. They are so easy, in fact, that you should have enough time to mix a jug of pre-dinner frivolity to really get the party started.

3 ripe bananas

100 ml/6½ tablespoons Irish cream liqueur (such as Bailey's)

2 tablespoons honey

100 g/3½ oz. milk chocolate, roughly chopped

CRUMBLE TOPPING

150 g/1 cup plus 2 tablespoons plain/all-purpose flour

100 g/1 stick minus 1 tablespoon cold unsalted butter, cubed

golden caster/natural cane sugar, for sprinkling

vanilla ice cream, to serve (optional)

6 small ramekins

SERVES 6

Preheat the oven to 190°C (375°F) Gas 5.

In a bowl, mash the bananas with the back of a spoon, then add the Irish cream and honey. Give the mixture a couple of good stirs, then divide between the ramekins (the mixture should come about two-thirds of the way up the dishes). Set aside while you make the crumble topping.

Put the flour and butter in a large mixing bowl and rub together with your fingers until the mixture resembles coarse breadcrumbs. It is best to use cool hands so that you don't overwork the mixture.

Sprinkle the crumble topping over the banana mixture, dividing it equally between the ramekins. Finally, sprinkle a little sugar on top of each crumble. Set the ramekins on a baking sheet and bake in the middle of the preheated oven for about 12–15 minutes until the topping is lightly golden. Serve immediately with vanilla ice-cream, if you like.

TIP If you're feeling a little more tropical, try substituting the Irish cream liqueur for coconut rum (such as Malibu) and adding 75 g/ ¾ cup of desiccated/shredded coconut to the crumble mix.

Jam jar crumbles
with amaretto cherries

100 g/½ cup caster/
  granulated sugar

170 g/½ cup honey

80 ml/⅓ cup amaretto,
  or other almond-flavoured
  liqueur

900 g/6 cups dark red cherries,
  pitted

CRUMBLE TOPPING

30 g/¼ cup plain/
  all-purpose flour

60 g/½ stick cold unsalted
  butter

2 tablespoons brown sugar

30 g/¼ cup ready-made
  granola

2 tablespoons ground almonds

mascarpone cream or vanilla
  ice cream, to serve

4 x 250-ml/1-cup glass jars

SERVES 4

Baking crumbles in glass jars has to be the best-kept secret around. Genius for outdoor entertaining and transporting to picnics, it is also a nostalgic nod to childhood, when everything seemed to be served in glass jars.

Combine the sugar, honey, amaretto and 700 ml/3 cups water in a saucepan and bring to the boil over a medium-high heat. Cook for about 8 minutes, until the sugar has dissolved. Reduce the heat and add the cherries. Simmer for 5 minutes, until the cherries plump up and are lightly cooked. Turn off the heat and let the cherries rest in the syrup for 5 minutes.

Preheat the oven to 190°C (375°F) Gas 5.

To make the crumble, place the flour, butter and sugar in a food processor and pulse until the mixture resembles coarse breadcrumbs. Stir in the granola and almonds and set aside.

Spoon the amaretto cherries equally between the glass jars and push the fruit down. Generously top the jars with the crumble, without pressing it down, and bake in the preheated oven for 20 minutes until the topping is golden brown.

Remove from the oven and serve with a big bowl of mascarpone cream or vanilla ice cream, if you like.

Strawberry crumble cups

Crumbles are an easy way to cook with seasonal fruit as well as a great way to use up sub-par fruit. The time in the oven will make it sweeter and softer and the nutty crumble topping adds a crunchy contrast in texture. Roasted strawberries, in particular, taste like straight-up candy – no extra sugar needed – making them the perfect base for a low-maintenance crumble. You can make a double batch of this crumble topping, store it in the freezer and use it to top seasonal fruit for when you want a fast dessert fix.

200 g/2 cups strawberries, sliced into 1.5-cm/½-inch thick pieces

CRUMBLE TOPPING

100 g/1 cup almond flour

50 g/½ cup rolled/old fashioned oats

½ teaspoon ground cinnamon

pinch of salt

60 ml/¼ cup gently melted coconut oil, plus extra for greasing

1 tablespoon maple syrup

whipped coconut cream or ice cream, to serve

4 small ramekins, greased with coconut oil

baking sheet, lined with foil or baking parchment

SERVES 4

Preheat the oven to 180°C (350°F) Gas 4.

Divide the strawberries between the ramekins, fitting them in snugly (they will reduce a little as they cook).

In a medium mixing bowl, combine the almond flour, oats, cinnamon and salt. Add the melted coconut oil and maple syrup and mix until everything is well coated. Divide the crumble mixture between the four greased ramekins.

Put the ramekins on the prepared baking tray and bake in the preheated oven for 30–35 minutes, until the strawberries are bubbling at the edges and the crumble toppings are golden and crisp.

Remove from the oven and leave to cool for 15–20 minutes before serving with whipped coconut cream or ice cream, as desired.

Plum crumble cheesecake

A delicious cheesecake and crumble hybrid, this crowd-pleasing dessert features cinnamon-roasted plums and a crumble base and topping.

800 g/1¾ lbs. red plums, halved and pitted

50 g/¼ cup caster/granulated sugar

2 teaspoons ground cinnamon

CRUMBLE

160 g/1½ sticks cold unsalted butter, cubed

200 g/1½ cups self-raising/self-rising flour

100 g/½ cup caster/granulated sugar

2 teaspoons ground cinnamon

CHEESECAKE FILLING

5 sheets leaf gelatine

300 g/1⅓ cups cream cheese

250 g/generous 1 cup ricotta

100 g/½ cup caster/granulated sugar

250 ml/1 cup double/heavy cream

23-cm/9-inch round springform cake pan, greased and lined with baking parchment

SERVES 12

Preheat the oven to 180°C (350°F) Gas 4.

Place the plums cut-side down in a roasting pan. Sprinkle with the sugar and cinnamon and add 100 ml/⅓ cup water to the pan. Bake in the preheated oven for 20–25 minutes until soft, then set aside to cool. Reserve 12 baked plum halves and the baking juices from the pan for the topping and purée the remaining plums in a food processor. (Leave the oven on for cooking the crumble.)

Prepare the crumble by rubbing the butter into the flour until the mixture resembles coarse breadcrumbs. Stir in the sugar and cinnamon and spread out over a large baking sheet. Bake for 10–15 minutes until the crumble is golden brown. Leave aside to cool then break the crumble into small pieces and sprinkle two-thirds of the crumble over the base of the prepared cake pan.

For the filling, soak the gelatine leaves in water until they are soft. In a large mixing bowl, whisk together the cream cheese, ricotta and sugar until smooth. Put the cream in a heatproof bowl set over a pan of simmering water and heat gently. Squeeze the water from the gelatine leaves and stir them into the warm cream until the gelatine has dissolved. Carefully add the gelatine cream to the cream cheese mixture. Pass it through a sieve/strainer to remove any gelatine pieces that have not dissolved. Beat the mixture until smooth and slightly thick, then stir in the plum purée. Pour the mixture over the crumble base and chill in the refrigerator for 3–4 hours or overnight until set.

To serve, place the reserved 12 plum halves on top of the cheesecake and drizzle over the reserved plum juice. Sprinkle the remaining crumble over the cheesecake to serve.

Caramel apple crisp

A cheat's way of making caramel is to melt caramel candies in butter, as this takes away all the worry of caramelizing sugar. Adding polenta/cornmeal to the crisp topping here gives it a lovely crunch. It looks very homely baked in a heavy cast-iron pan but an ordinary ovenproof dish is fine too.

6 tart eating apples,
  such as Cox's or
  Granny Smith

freshly squeezed juice of
  ½ lemon

50 g/3½ tablespoons unsalted
  butter

100 g/3½ oz. hard caramel
  sweets/candies, crushed
  or chopped

pinch of ground cinnamon

OAT CRISP TOPPING

85 g/generous ½ cup fine
  polenta/cornmeal

85 g/¾ cup rolled/old
  fashioned oats

130 g/⅔ cup demerara/
  turbinado sugar

80 g/¾ stick unsalted butter,
  melted

chilled crème fraîche or ice
  cream, to serve (optional)

*cast-iron frying pan/skillet
  or ovenproof dish*

SERVES 6

Preheat the oven to 190°C (375°F) Gas 5.

Peel, core and thickly slice the apples and toss them with the lemon juice. Melt the butter in the cast-iron frying pan/skillet that will go in the oven or a heavy-bottomed frying pan/skillet, then add the crushed hard caramel sweets/candies. Stir until melted, add the apples and cinnamon and toss well to coat in the buttery caramel. Remove from the heat and set aside.

To make the oat crisp topping, put the polenta/cornmeal, oats and sugar in a bowl and mix well. Stir in the melted butter and work through the mixture with your fingertips until it resembles coarse breadcrumbs.

Lightly sprinkle the topping mixture evenly over the surface of the apples in the pan (or transfer the apples to the ovenproof dish first if needed), mounding them up a little towards the centre. Bake in the preheated oven for 40 minutes, until the topping is brown and crisp. Serve warm with crème fraîche or ice cream, as preferred.

Mango and coconut macaroon crisp

This is a back-to-front crumble. The crumble and mango are baked separately, then served together for maximum crunch. You can prepare the topping in bulk and store it in an airtight container so that you can make a really exotic dessert at a moment's notice. Do serve coconut ice cream with this, if you can find it.

2 ripe mangoes

finely grated zest and freshly squeezed juice of 1 lime

COCONUT MACAROON TOPPING

2 tablespoons wholemeal/whole-wheat flour

40 g/3 tablespoons unsalted butter

40 g/1/2 cup unsweetened desiccated/dried coconut

80 g/3 oz. coconut macaroon biscuits/cookies

40 g/3 1/4 tablespoons demerara/turbinado sugar

coconut or vanilla ice cream, to serve (optional)

4 small, shallow ovenproof dishes

SERVES 4

Preheat the oven to 200°C (400°F) Gas 6.

Peel the mangoes and slice the sides away as near to the pit as possible, then chop the flesh. Toss this with the lime zest and juice and spoon into 4 individual baking dishes (these must be shallow, as the mango needs to go into something that heats through quite quickly). Put them on a baking sheet and cook in the preheated oven for about 15 minutes.

Meanwhile, make the topping by rubbing together the flour, butter and coconut with your fingers until it resembles coarse breadcrumbs. Lightly crush the macaroon biscuits/cookies in a plastic bag, then stir these into the coconut mixture along with the sugar. Spread out onto a non-stick baking sheet and put in the oven with the mango. Toast the topping for 10–15 minutes, until crisp. Remove both trays from the oven and sprinkle the toasted coconut macaroon topping over the hot mango.

Serve immediately with coconut or vanilla ice cream, if liked.

Peach cobbler

8 firm but ripe peaches,
  peeled and pitted

50 g/¼ cup light muscovado
  sugar

COBBLER TOPPING

450 g/3½ cups self-raising/
  rising flour

½ teaspoon salt

220 g/2 sticks cold unsalted
  butter, cubed

140 g/¾ cup caster/
  granulated sugar

seeds of 1 vanilla pod/bean

260 ml/1 generous cup
  buttermilk

vanilla ice cream or custard,
  to serve (optional)

medium ovenproof dish

SERVES 6–8

Rustic, homely and filling, this peach cobbler makes a
comforting end to any meal. This is delicious family food
at its best – satisfying and perfect for sharing. If you can't
get hold of peaches, you can use whatever fruit is in season.
Plums, cherries and apples all work particularly well.

Preheat the oven to 190°C (375°F) Gas 5.

Slice the peaches and arrange them in an even layer in the dish,
then sprinkle over the sugar.

In a large mixing bowl, sift together the flour and salt and rub
in the butter with your fingers. Stir through the sugar and vanilla
and then add the buttermilk. Beat together with a wooden
spoon until fully incorporated.

Drop mounds of dough off a tablespoon on top of the peaches
to create a cobblestone effect. Bake in the preheated oven for
25–30 minutes, or until the top is golden and the fruit is soft.
Serve hot with vanilla ice cream or custard, as preferred.

Blueberry and lemon cobbler

675 g/5¼ cups blueberries

COBBLER TOPPING

120 g/1⅛ sticks butter, at room temperature

75 g/⅓ cup caster/granulated sugar

finely grated zest and freshly squeezed juice of 1 lemon

100 ml/scant ½ cup soured cream

75 g/½ cup plain/all-purpose flour

75 g/½ cup fine polenta/cornmeal

3 teaspoons baking powder

½ teaspoon salt

2 tablespoons honey

50 g/¼ cup caster/granulated sugar

vanilla ice cream, to serve (optional)

medium ovenproof dish, buttered

SERVES 4

Dark bubbling blueberries hide under a light cobbled crust of lemony polenta cake. The secret of this dish is not to spoon the blobs of topping mixture too closely together – leaving a little space around each one allows the fruit to bubble up through the gaps.

Preheat oven to 180°C (350°F) Gas 4.

Spread the blueberries out in the buttered ovenproof dish. Cream 100 g/1 stick plus 1 tablespoon of the butter with the sugar and lemon zest, until pale and fluffy. Beat in the soured cream. Sift the flour with the polenta/cornmeal, baking powder and salt and fold into the cream mixture.

Dot small spoonfuls of the mixture over the blueberries in a very random manner, until the top of the dish has been covered, leaving about 2.5 cm/1 inch of space around each one. (This will give the dish its cobbled look, and the juices from the fruit will bubble up around the dough.) Bake in the preheated oven for about 20 minutes, until the top is firm. While the cobbler is baking, prepare the butter mixture for the crust.

Put the remaining butter in a small saucepan with the honey, lemon juice and sugar and melt over a low heat. Remove the cobbler from the oven and pour this mixture over the crust.

Increase the oven temperature to 190°C (375°F) Gas 5. Return the cobbler to the oven and cook for a further 15–20 minutes, until golden. Serve warm with vanilla ice cream, if liked.

Pies and tarts

Classic apple pie

Crisp, buttery pastry with piles of cinnamon and vanilla-scented apple –
there are few desserts more comforting than this. Here, a combination of
dessert and cooking apples is used to balance the sharpness of the fruit.

SHORTCRUST PASTRY

280 g/generous 2 cups plain/
all-purpose flour

pinch of salt

115 g/1 stick cold unsalted
butter, cubed

1 egg, beaten

PIE FILLING

4 cooking apples and 4 dessert
apples, peeled and cored

freshly squeezed juice of
1 lemon

2 teaspoons ground cinnamon

60 g/generous ¼ cup soft
light brown sugar

115 g/generous ½ cup caster/
granulated sugar, plus extra
for sprinkling

2 tablespoons plain/all-purpose
flour, plus extra for dusting

1 teaspoon pure vanilla extract

pinch of salt

60 g/½ stick unsalted butter,
cubed

custard or cream, to serve
(optional)

23-cm/9-inch deep pie dish,
greased

SERVES 6–8

Preheat the oven to 200°C (400°F) Gas 6.

Sift the flour into a mixing bowl and add the salt. Use your fingertips to rub the butter into the flour until it resembles breadcrumbs. Mix in 1-2 tablespoons cold water with a round-bladed knife. Bring the dough together into a ball, adding a little more water if needed. Wrap the pastry in clingfilm/plastic wrap and refrigerate for 1 hour.

Meanwhile, cut all the apples into slices and stir together with the lemon juice in a bowl. Add the cinnamon, sugars, flour, vanilla extract and salt and toss together with your hands to mix.

Divide the pastry in half, one slightly larger than the other. On a lightly floured surface, roll out the larger half of the pastry into a circle just larger than the size of your pie dish. Using the rolling pin to help lift it, transfer the pastry to line the pie dish, gently pressing in so that it fits snugly. Brush the inside of the pastry with some of the beaten egg to prevent it becoming soggy. Place the apples into the pastry case and dot with the cubes of butter. Brush the outer edge of the pastry case with a little beaten egg.

Roll out the remaining pastry into a circle just larger than your pie dish and place over the apples. Press together the edges of the pastry base and lid with your fingers to seal. If you want to create a pretty pattern, roll a patterned pastry tool around the edge. Trim away any excess pastry using a knife. You can re-roll this out and cut out leaf shapes to decorate the top of your pie, if you wish.

Brush the top of the pie with beaten egg and sprinkle with sugar. Cut a slit in the top of the pie to let any steam escape during cooking. Bake in the preheated oven for 15 minutes, then reduce the temperature to 170°C (340°F) Gas 3 and bake for about 45 minutes more, until the pastry is golden brown and the apples are soft. Remove from the oven and leave to cool for about 15 minutes, then serve with custard or cream, as you prefer.

Individual apple and sultana pies

PIE CRUST

1 quantity Shortcrust Pastry (see page 42)

1 egg, beaten

sugar, for sprinkling

PIE FILLING

80 g/^{2}/$_3$ cup sultanas/golden raisins and chopped dried figs

3 tablespoons dark rum

30 g/2^1/$_2$ tablespoons soft light brown sugar

^{1}/$_2$ teaspoon mixed spice/apple pie spice

125 g/1^1/$_8$ sticks softened unsalted butter, plus extra for spreading

6 eating apples, peeled and cored

6 small bay leaves and 6 thin shards of cinnamon stick

6 small pie dishes or ramekins

SERVES 6

Rum-soaked dried fruit is stuffed inside the whole apple filling for each of these little darling pies. With a bay leaf and a sliver of cinnamon acting as a stalk, the decoration reminds us of what is buried under the pastry!

Put the sultanas/golden raisins and figs into a screw-top jar with the rum. Shake and leave to soak for at least 2 hours or overnight.

Prepare the pastry as instructed and refrigerate for 1 hour.

Meanwhile, mix the soaked fruit with the sugar, mixed/apple pie spice and butter. Spoon the spiced fruit and butter mixture into the holes in the cored apples, pressing in with the handle of a teaspoon. Spread a little more butter over the apples. Carefully place each apple into a dish or ramekin into which it fits snugly, protruding above the top edge, but not touching the sides.

Roll out the pastry and cut out 6 circles a good bit larger than the diameter of the dishes. Brush the rims of the dishes with a little water and set a circle of pastry on top of each dish, gently moulding over each apple. Press the edges of the pastry to the rim to seal and cut a tiny slit in the top of each pie to let the steam escape.Use any pastry trimmings to cut shapes to decorate the top of the pies if you like, then refrigerate for 20 minutes before brushing with beaten egg and sprinkling with sugar.

Preheat the oven to 200°C (400°F) Gas 6.

Set the pies on a baking sheet and bake in the preheated oven for 15 minutes. Reduce the temperature to 150°C (300°F) Gas 2 and stick a bay leaf and cinnamon shard into the steam holes. Bake for a further 40 minutes until the apples are soft but not collapsing. (If they look like they are browning too much, cover with foil.) Remove from the oven and leave to cool for about 15 minutes, then serve.

CHEDDAR PIE CRUST

400 g/3 cups plain/
  all-purpose flour

$\frac{1}{2}$ teaspoon salt

225 g/2 sticks unsalted cold
  butter, cubed

225 g/8 oz. Cheddar, grated

60 ml/$\frac{1}{4}$ cup each iced water
  and white vinegar, mixed

1 egg, beaten

1 tablespoon mixed sugar
  and salt

SALTED CARAMEL SAUCE

200 g/1 cup caster/
  granulated sugar

115 g/1 stick unsalted butter

120 ml/$\frac{1}{2}$ cup double/
  heavy cream

1$\frac{1}{2}$ teaspoons fine sea salt

PIE FILLING

5–6 medium–large apples

squeezed juice of 1 lemon

65 g/$\frac{1}{3}$ cup golden caster/
  natural cane sugar

2 tablespoons plain/
  all-purpose flour

$\frac{1}{4}$ teaspoon each ground
  cinnamon and ground allspice

STREUSEL TOPPING

150 g/$\frac{3}{4}$ cup white sugar

100 g/$\frac{3}{4}$ cup plain/
  all-purpose flour

1 tablespoon iced water

1$\frac{1}{2}$ teaspoons ground cinnamon

70 g/$\frac{1}{2}$ stick unsalted butter

23-cm/9-inch pie dish

SERVES 8

Apple cheddar pie

This delicious pie is something everyone should try once!

To make the pie crust, combine the flour and salt in a mixing bowl. Use your fingertips to rub in the butter until the mixture resembles coarse breadcrumbs. Stir in the cheese. Gradually stir in the water and vinegar until the dough comes together. Divide the dough into two balls, one slightly larger than the other, and wrap in clingfilm/plastic wrap. Refrigerate for 4 hours or overnight. Roll the larger ball out on a lightly floured surface. Using your rolling pin to help lift it, transfer the pastry to line the pie dish, gently pressing it in and trimming any edges. Roll the other ball out on a piece of baking parchment for your pie top. Refrigerate both until needed.

To make the salted caramel sauce, heat the sugar and 80 ml/$\frac{1}{4}$ cup water together in a small saucepan set over a low heat until just dissolved. Add the butter and boil slowly for about an hour until the mixture turns a deep, golden brown. Once the mixture is ready, remove it from the heat and immediately add the cream – it will bubble rapidly so take care. Whisk the caramel together over a low heat and sprinkle in the sea salt. Set aside until needed.

Core, peel and thinly slice the apples for the filling and toss with the lemon juice in a bowl. Sprinkle the sugar, flour, cinnamon, and allspice over the apples and toss together.

Preheat the oven to 190°C (375°F) Gas 5.

Put one-third of the apple slices in the base of the pastry-lined dish and pour over one-third of the caramel. Repeat the apple and caramel layers twice more until both are used up. Assemble the lattice crust (if doing). Brush the crust with beaten egg and sprinkle with the sugar-salt mixture. Put the pie on a baking sheet and bake in the preheated oven for 20 minutes. Reduce the temperature to 170°C (340°F) Gas 3 and bake for a further 25–35 minutes until the pastry is golden. Let cool for at least 30 minutes while you make the streusel topping. Soften the butter, then mix all the ingredients until crumbly and spread on a baking sheet. Bake for 15–20 minutes in an oven preheated to 175°C (350°F) Gas 4 until golden. Let cool briefly and then use to top the pie.

Buttered cider apple pie

PIE CRUST

1 quantity Shortcrust Pastry (see page 42)

PIE FILLING

2 large cooking apples, peeled, cored and roughly grated

finely grated zest and freshly squeezed juice of 1 tangerine, or similar

75 g/5 tablespoons golden caster/natural cane sugar, plus 2 tablespoons for sprinkling

75 g/5 tablespoons unsalted butter, melted

2 tablespoons apple cider, apple brandy or Calvados

1 egg, beaten

20-cm/8-inch pie dish

pie funnel

SERVES 4

This delectable twist on the classic combines cider, apples and butter with a hint of tangerine. Grating the cooking apples makes a soft filling, which really melts in the mouth and is so easy to prepare. Cooking apples (such as Bramley apples), which are more tart, work best in this recipe.

Prepare the pastry as instructed and refrigerate for 1 hour.

Preheat the oven to 200°C (400°F) Gas 6 and set a heavy baking sheet on the middle shelf.

Divide the pastry into two balls, one slightly larger. Roll the larger ball of pastry out on a lightly floured surface. Using your rolling pin to help lift it, transfer the pastry to line the pie dish, gently pressing it in. Set the pie funnel in the middle of the pie dish.

Put the grated apple in a mixing bowl and add the tangerine zest and juice, sugar, 50 g/4 tablespoons of the melted butter (keep the remainder warm), the cider or brandy and the beaten egg. Mix well and spoon into the lined pie dish, levelling the surface.

Brush the edges of the pastry in the pie dish with water. Roll out the remaining pastry to a round slightly larger than the pie dish. Make a hole in the middle of the remaining pastry and, using a rolling pin, lift it up and drape over the pie dish, making sure that the hole drops over the pie funnel. Press together the edges of the pastry base and lid with your fingers. Trim off the excess pastry and use pastry cutters to cut shapes from it and use them to decorate the top of the pie, if desired.

Set the pie on the baking sheet in the preheated oven and bake for 15 minutes. Reduce the temperature to 190°C (375°F) Gas 5 and bake for a further 15 minutes. Remove from the oven and brush with the remaining melted butter, sprinkle with the 2 tablespoons of sugar and bake for a further 10–15 minutes until the pastry is golden brown. Leave to cool a little before serving.

Classic tarte tatin

Tarte tatin is one of the most popular French desserts – is there anyone who doesn't like caramelized apples with buttery puff pastry? Serve with Calvados cream or crème fraîche for a perfect dessert with friends. The exact number of apples needed will depend on how large your apples are and the size of your pan.

160 g/generous ¾ cup caster/granulated sugar, plus extra for sprinkling

90 g/¾ stick unsalted butter

pinch of salt

5–7 small dessert apples

freshly squeezed juice of 1 large lemon

plain/all-purpose flour, for dusting

500 g/18 oz. ready-made puff pastry

1 tablespoon whole milk

Calvados cream or crème fraîche, to serve (optional)

20-cm/8-inch tatin pan or pie dish

SERVES 6–8

In a heavy-based saucepan, heat the sugar until it melts and turns golden brown. Do not stir, but swirl the pan to move the sugar to prevent it from burning. Watch closely as the sugar melts, as it can easily burn. Once caramelized, add the butter and salt to the pan, whisking as it melts. Pour into the base of the tatin pan or pie dish and leave to cool.

Preheat the oven to 200°C (400°F) Gas 6.

Peel and core the apples and cut into quarters. Toss the apples with the lemon juice in a bowl to prevent them discolouring. Place the apples closely together in the pan on top of the caramel.

On a lightly floured surface, roll the pastry out to about 5 mm/¼ inch thick and cut out a circle of pastry that is about 1 cm/½ inch larger than your pan. Place the pastry over the apples and tuck it down at the sides of the pan so that the apples are encased. Brush the top of the pastry with milk and sprinkle with a little sugar.

Bake in the preheated oven for 20–30 minutes, until the pastry has risen and is golden brown. Remove from the oven, allow to cool for a few minutes, then carefully invert the pan onto a plate, taking care that you do not burn yourself on the hot caramel. It is best to do this by placing the plate upside-down on top of the pan, then, holding both tightly with oven gloves or a kitchen cloth, very quickly turn over, so that the pie ends up apple-side up on your serving plate.

Serve immediately while still warm with the accompaniment of your choosing. This pie is best eaten straight away.

Blueberry pie

The aroma of this classic pie when you remove it from the oven is so heavenly, you might find that it takes a lot of willpower to resist digging in immediately with a spoon! You can serve it warm with cream or custard, but it is also nice served cold on its own.

PIE CRUST

plain/all-purpose flour, for dusting

500 g/18 oz. ready-made puff pastry

1 egg, beaten

PIE FILLING

600 g/5 cups fresh blueberries

freshly squeezed juice and grated zest of 2 lemons

100 g/½ cup caster/granulated sugar, plus extra for sprinkling

2 tablespoons cornflour/cornstarch, sifted

23-cm/9-inch pie dish, greased

SERVES 6-8

Preheat the oven to 200°C (400°F) Gas 6.

On a lightly floured surface, roll out the pastry thinly until it is a circle about 6 cm/2½ inches larger than the size of your pie dish. Using the rolling pin to help lift it, move the pastry into the pie dish and gently press it down so that it fits snugly inside with some of the pastry hanging over the top edge. Brush the inside of the pastry case with some of the beaten egg using a pastry brush. This will help prevent the pastry from becoming soggy.

Place the blueberries, lemon juice and zest, sugar and cornflour/cornstarch in a bowl. Stir well so that everything is mixed together.

Spoon the blueberry mixture into the pie dish, piling it high in the centre. Lift the edges of the pastry up over the blueberries and crimp together with your fingers to make a decorative pattern. The centre of the pie should remain open so that you can see the blueberries.

Brush the top of the pastry with the remaining beaten egg and sprinkle with sugar. Bake the pie in the preheated oven for 40–50 minutes, until the pastry is crisp and golden brown.

Remove from the oven and leave to cool slightly, if serving warm, to allow the sauce to thicken. Alternatively, leave to cool completely and serve cold.

Diner-style cherry pie

Cherry pie is one of the world's most beloved treats and a staple of any good, red-blooded diner. It's best served with ice cream or à la mode.

FUSS-FREE PIE CRUST

340 g/2½ cups plain/
  all-purpose flour

1 teaspoon fine sea salt

230 g/2 sticks cold unsalted
  butter, cut into small pieces

60–120 ml/¼–½ cup iced
  water

1 egg beaten with
  2 tablespoons water or milk

1 tablespoon caster/granulated
  sugar, for sprinkling

PIE FILLING

600 g/4 cups fresh sweet
  cherries, such as Merchant
  or Bing, pitted

200–300 g/1–1½ cups
  granulated sugar

4 tablespoons cornflour/
  cornstarch

½ tablespoon almond extract

*23-cm/9-inch shallow pie dish,
  greased*

*baking sheet lined with
  baking parchment*

SERVES 8

In a food processor, combine the flour and salt and pulse briefly. Add the butter and pulse until the mixture resembles coarse breadcrumbs, with a few pea-size pieces of butter remaining. Sprinkle with 60 ml/¼ cup iced water. Pulse until the dough is crumbly but holds together when squeezed. If necessary, add the extra water a little at a time. Divide and shape the dough into two 2-cm/1-inch thick discs, one slightly larger than the other, and wrap in clingfilm/plastic wrap. Refrigerate for at least 1 hour.

Let the pastry come to room temperature when ready to bake. On a lightly floured surface, roll the larger disc out into a 33–35 cm/ 13–14 inch round and the smaller one into a 30.5 cm/12 inch round. Using your rolling pin to help lift it, transfer the larger disc of pastry to line the pie dish. Gently press it in so that it fits snugly. Place the smaller pastry disc on the prepared baking sheet. Refrigerate both for 15 minutes, while you make the filling.

Put the cherries in a large saucepan, place over a low heat and cover. After the cherries release their juices, which may take a few minutes, mix the sugar and cornflour/cornstarch together, tip into the hot cherries and mix well. Continue cooking over a low heat until the juice is thickened and translucent. Remove from the heat, then stir in the almond extract and leave to cool completely.

Preheat the oven to 190°C (375°F) Gas 5. Moisten the rim of the pie shell with the beaten egg mixture. Spoon the cooled cherry filling into the pie. Cover the filling with the top crust and press the edges together with your fingers or the tines of a fork to seal, trimming away any overhanging edges. Brush the top crust with the rest of the egg wash and sprinkle with sugar. Cut slits in the dough to form a star shape and let the steam escape. Bake the pie in the preheated oven for 50 minutes until the crust is golden brown. Leave the pie to cool before serving or keep at room temperature and serve the next day.

Lattice-topped Morello cherry pie

Children and adults alike will love this lusciously sweet Morello cherry pie, it's impossible to just have one slice!

AMERICAN CREAM CHEESE PIE CRUST

300 g/2⅓ cups plain/all-purpose flour

2 tablespoons icing/confectioners' sugar

large pinch of salt

175 g/1½ sticks unsalted butter, chilled and diced

175 g/¾ cup cream cheese

4–6 tablespoons whole milk, chilled, plus extra to glaze

PIE FILLING

3 x 350-g/12-oz. packs frozen pitted Morello cherries (or 1 kg/2¼ lbs., drained weight, canned Morello cherries)

200 g/1 cup caster/granulated sugar, plus extra for sprinkling

½ teaspoon ground cinnamon or a good pinch of allspice

freshly squeezed juice of 1 lemon

5 tablespoons cornflour/cornstarch

23-cm/9-inch shallow pie dish

baking sheet lined with baking parchment

SERVES 6

To make the pastry, sift the flour into a mixing bowl with the icing/confectioners' sugar and salt. Rub in the butter and cream cheese with your fingertips until the mixture resembles coarse breadcrumbs. Mix in enough of the milk until the dough comes together into a ball. Knead very briefly until smooth. Divide into two pieces, one slightly larger than the other, then wrap in clingfilm/plastic wrap and refrigerate for 1 hour.

To make the filling, mix the cherries with all the remaining ingredients and leave to stand for 20 minutes, then stir once more.

Preheat the oven to 220°C (425°F) Gas 7.

On a lightly floured surface, roll out the larger half of the pastry. Using your rolling pin to help lift it, transfer the pastry to line the pie dish and gently press it in so that it fits snugly. Roll out the second half of the dough into a rectangle and cut into strips long enough to drape over the pie. Put the strips onto the prepared baking sheet and refrigerate.

Spoon the cherries into the lined pie dish, mounding them up in the centre. Brush the edges of the pastry with water, then lay the pastry strips on top, weaving them to form a lattice. Trim the edges, then crimp to seal. Brush the top with milk and sprinkle with sugar.

Set the pie on a baking sheet to catch any juices and bake in the preheated oven for 20 minutes. Reduce the oven temperature to 180°C (350°F) Gas 4 and bake for a further 30–40 minutes until the thickened cherry juices bubble up through the lattice. Cover the top loosely with kitchen foil if the pastry looks as if it is browning too quickly. Serve warm or cold.

TIP This pie is very juicy – you may want to keep some juices back and boil separately to thicken them.

Rhubarb and mascarpone tart

TART FILLING

500 g/18 oz. rhubarb,
cut into 2-cm/1-inch slices

175 g/¾ cup caster/
granulated sugar

30 g/2 tablespoons salted
butter, softened

225 g/scant 1 cup mascarpone

30 g/¼ cup plain/
all-purpose flour

grated zest of 1 orange

2 eggs, separated

100 ml/scant ½ cup double/
heavy cream

SHORTBREAD BASE

135 g/9 tablespoons salted
butter, softened

65 g/⅓ cup caster/granulated
sugar

160 g/1¼ cups plain/
all-purpose flour

15 g/2 tablespoons cornflour/
cornstarch

25 g/3 tablespoons rice flour

SYRUP

2 teaspoons arrowroot powder

freshly squeezed juice of
1 orange

23-cm/9-inch loose-based
tart pan

baking beans

SERVES 8–10

The pleasing sharpness of the fruit contrasts wonderfully well with the creamy mascarpone filling in this tart.

Preheat the oven to 190°C (375°F) Gas 5.

Put the rhubarb in an ovenproof dish and sprinkle with 60 g/⅓ cup of the sugar. Cover with foil and roast in the preheated oven for about 15 minutes. Remove the rhubarb from the oven and strain it, reserving the juices for later. Set aside. Leave the oven on.

To make the base, put the ingredients into a mixing bowl and rub together using your fingertips to form a paste. Knead gently into a smooth ball of dough. Alternatively, blend the ingredients in a food processor to form a smooth dough. Roll it out on a lightly floured surface into a circle a little larger than the pan. Using your rolling pin to help lift it, transfer the dough to the tart pan. Gently press it in and trim away any overhanging edges. Line the pastry with baking parchment and fill with baking beans. Blind bake in the preheated oven for 15–20 minutes. Take out of the oven, then remove the parchment and baking beans and leave to cool. When cool, line the sides of the tart pan with strips of baking parchment about 5 cm/2 inches high.

To make the tart filling, beat together the butter, remaining sugar, mascarpone, flour and orange zest in a large bowl. Add the egg yolks and cream. Beat to a creamy consistency and set aside.

Put the egg whites into a very clean bowl and use an electric whisk to beat on high speed until soft peaks form. Whisk the egg whites into the mascarpone mixture, then spoon into the tart case. Scatter over the roasted rhubarb and bake in the preheated oven for 40–45 minutes or until the filling is set but with a slight wobble.

To make the syrup, stir together the arrowroot and 2 tablespoons water in a cup. Put the reserved rhubarb juice and the orange juice into a saucepan and bring to the boil. Remove from the heat and gradually stir in the arrowroot until the syrup is slightly thickened (you may not need it all). The syrup will thicken further as it cools. Serve the tart warm with the syrup poured on top.

Pile high peach pie

Fruit pies should always be bursting with filling and this pie is a perfect example. It is best made with ripe peaches when they are in season. The pretty heart shapes cut into the crust create an attractive finish.

PIE CRUST

1 quantity Shortcrust Pastry (see page 42)

plain/all-purpose flour, for dusting

1 egg, beaten

PIE FILLING

8 ripe peaches, pitted

2 tablespoons cornflour/ cornstarch, sifted

70 g/6 tablespoons caster/ granulated sugar, plus extra for sprinkling

1/2 teaspoon vanilla salt (or 1/2 teaspoon salt plus 1/2 teaspoon vanilla extract)

23-cm/9-inch deep pie dish, greased

SERVES 6–8

Prepare the pastry as instructed and refrigerate for 1 hour.

Preheat the oven to 200°C (400°F) Gas 6.

Roll out one-half of the pastry on a lightly floured surface into a circle just larger than the size of your pie dish. Using the rolling pin to help lift it, carefully transfer the pastry to the pie dish and gently press it down so that it fits snugly. Brush the inside of the pastry with some of the beaten egg, this will help prevent the pastry from becoming soggy.

Cut the peaches into thick slices and place in a bowl with the corn flour/cornstarch, sugar and vanilla salt. Toss so that the peaches are coated evenly. Pile the peaches into the pie case.

Roll the remaining pastry out into a circle slightly larger than the size of the dish. Cut out some heart shapes from the centre of the pastry, and reserve the pastry hearts. Brush the edges of the bottom pastry layer with a little beaten egg, then place the second pastry circle on top, so that you can see the filling through the heart-shaped holes. Crimp the edges of the pastry together with your fingertips or with the prongs of a fork, trimming away excess pastry. Brush the top of the pastry with the remaining egg and stick the pastry hearts decoratively on the top, brushing the hearts with a little more beaten egg. Sprinkle with sugar.

Bake in the preheated oven for 30–40 minutes, until the pastry is golden brown. This pie is best eaten on the day it is made, although it can be stored in the refrigerator and eaten the following day if you wish.

Nectarine crumble tart

If you can't decide between a tart or a crumble, this dessert is the best of both worlds. Bursting with juicy fruit and topped with a crumble made from marzipan and amaretti biscuits/cookies, this tart is a real treat.

TART CRUST

1 quantity Shortcrust Pastry (see page 42)

plain/all-purpose flour, for dusting

1 egg, beaten

TART FILLING

6 ripe nectarines

100 g/$\frac{1}{2}$ cup caster/granulated sugar

2 tablespoons cornflour/cornstarch

$\frac{1}{2}$ teaspoon salt

1 teaspoon vanilla pod/bean powder or pure vanilla extract

CRUMBLE TOPPING

150 g/5$\frac{1}{2}$ oz. amaretti biscuits/cookies

130 g/4$\frac{1}{2}$ oz. golden marzipan

100 g/1 stick minus 1 tablespoon unsalted butter, melted

icing/confectioners' sugar, for dusting

cream, to serve (optional)

23-cm/9-inch tart pan, greased

SERVES 8–10

Prepare the pastry as instructed and refrigerate for 1 hour.

Roll out the pastry on a lightly floured surface into a circle just larger than the size of your tart pan. Using your rolling pin to help lift it, transfer the pastry to line the tart pan. Press it in so that it fits snugly and trim away any overhanging edges. Use the trimmings to create a decorative border, if you like, and stick it to the edge using a little beaten egg. Prick the base with a fork and refrigerate for 30 minutes.

Preheat the oven to 180°C (350°F) Gas 4.

To make the crumble topping, crush the amaretti into small pieces with your hands and put into a bowl. Chop the marzipan into small pieces and add to the crushed amaretti. Stir in the warm melted butter and squash the mixture together with your hands so that everything is mixed well and has the texture of a crumble.

To make the filling, remove the pits from the nectarines and chop the flesh into large chunks. Place in a mixing bowl with the sugar, cornflour/cornstarch, salt and vanilla and stir together. Brush the bottom of the pastry with a thin layer of beaten egg and then place the nectarines on top. Sprinkle over the crumble topping.

Bake in the preheated oven for 30–40 minutes, until the pastry is golden brown. If the crumble topping starts to turn dark, then cover loosely with foil. Serve warm or cold with cream and dusted with icing/confectioners' sugar, if you like.

Apricot and vanilla tart

APRICOTS

16 apricots, halved and pits removed

50 g/¼ cup caster/granulated sugar

freshly squeezed juice of 1 lemon

50 g/3½ tablespoons unsalted butter

TART CRUST

1 quantity Shortcrust Pastry (see page 42)

plain/all-purpose flour, for dusting

TART FILLING

250 g/generous 1 cup mascarpone cheese

150 ml/⅔ cup crème fraîche

100 g/3½ oz. vanilla custard

½ teaspoon vanilla bean powder or 1 teaspoon vanilla extract

1 heaped tablespoon icing/confectioners' sugar, sifted

GLAZE

2 tablespoons apricot glaze or apricot jam/jelly

freshly squeezed juice of 1 lemon

23-cm/9-inch loose-bottom, fluted tart pan, greased

baking beans

SERVES 8

When roasted with a little butter, sugar and lemon juice, apricots become the perfect tart topping. This is a great dessert to serve on sunny days when apricots are in abundance.

Prepare the pastry as instructed and refrigerate for 1 hour.

Preheat the oven to 180°C (350°F) Gas 4.

Place the apricots, cut-side down, in a roasting pan and sprinkle with the sugar and lemon juice. Add the butter and bake for 15–20 minutes, until the fruit is just soft. Remove from the oven and leave to cool. Increase the temperature to 200°C (400°F) Gas 6.

Roll out the pastry on a lightly floured surface into a circle just larger than the size of your tart pan. Using the rolling pin to help lift it, carefully move the pastry into the pan and press it down so that it fits snugly. Leave some pastry hanging over the edge of the pan, this will be trimmed neatly after the tart is baked. Prick the base with a fork and refrigerate for 30 minutes.

Line the pastry case with baking parchment, fill with baking beans and bake blind for about 20–25 minutes in the centre of the preheated oven, until the pastry is golden brown. Remove the baking beans and parchment and trim the edge of the pastry with a sharp knife by running it along the top of the pan.

Blitz one-third of the apricots and the cooking syrup to a purée in a food processor and strain so that the purée is smooth. In a bowl, whisk together the apricot purée, mascarpone cheese, crème fraîche, custard, vanilla and icing/confectioners' sugar until smooth. Spoon the mixture into the tart crust and spread out. Place the remaining apricots on top of the filling, moving them carefully with a spatula so that they retain their shape.

In a saucepan, heat the apricot glaze and lemon juice until melted. Leave to cool slightly, then brush over the top of the fruit. Leave to cool, then refrigerate for at least 2 hours before serving.

Rustic plum tart

If you are lucky enough to have a plum tree in your garden, then making this plum tart with a glut of fresh plums is so satisfying. You can use a few different varieties to create a more decorative coloured pattern, if you wish.

TART CRUST

500 g/18 oz. ready-made puff pastry

plain/all-purpose flour, for dusting

1 egg, beaten

TART FILLING

100 g/3½ oz. golden marzipan, coarsely grated

100 g/1 cup ground almonds

50 g/¼ cup caster/granulated sugar, plus extra to sprinkle

about 16–18 plums

GLAZE

2 tablespoons apricot glaze or apricot jam/jelly

whipped cream, to serve (optional)

20-cm/8-inch square, loose-bottom, tart pan, greased

SERVES 6–8

Preheat the oven to 200°C (400°F) Gas 6.

Roll out the pastry on a lightly floured surface into a square that is about 6 cm/2¼ inches larger than the size of your pan. Using the rolling pin to help lift it, carefully transfer the pastry into the tart pan and gently press it down so that it fits snugly into the corners. Brush the inside of the pastry case with some of the beaten egg to prevent the pastry from becoming soggy.

In a bowl stir together the grated marzipan, ground almonds and sugar. Sprinkle into the pastry case in an even layer.

Cut the plums into quarters and remove the pits. Place the plum quarters in rows in the pan in a decorative pattern. Pull the pastry edges up around the side of the plums. Brush the pastry with the remaining beaten egg and sprinkle the fruit and pastry with a little extra sugar.

Bake the tart in the preheated oven for 30–40 minutes, until the pastry has puffed up and is golden brown and the fruit still holds its shape but has released some of its juices. Remove from the oven.

Heat the apricot glaze or jam/jelly in a saucepan and then brush over the warm plums to glaze. Serve immediately warm or cold with whipped cream, if liked.

Pear and cranberry pie

Cranberries and pears are a great combination, and this festive pie decorated with stars and snowflakes is a comforting treat and a good alternative to other rich desserts often eaten in the holiday season. You can use frozen or dried cranberries if fresh cranberries are not available.

PIE CRUST

1 quantity Shortcrust Pastry (see page 42)

plain/all-purpose flour, for dusting

1 egg, beaten

PIE FILLING

10 ripe pears

freshly squeezed juice of 1 lemon

150 g/generous 1½ cups fresh cranberries

2 teaspoons ground cinnamon

150 g/¾ cup caster/granulated sugar, plus extra for sprinkling

2 tablespoons plain/all-purpose flour, plus extra for dusting

pinch of salt

60 g/½ stick unsalted butter, cubed

custard or cream, to serve (optional)

23-cm/9-inch pie dish, greased

snowflake and star cutters (optional)

SERVES 8

Prepare the pastry as instructed and refrigerate for 1 hour.

Preheat the oven to 200°C (400°F) Gas 6.

Divide the pastry in two, with one piece slightly bigger than the other. Roll the slightly larger piece out on a lightly floured surface into a circle just larger than your pie dish. Using your rolling pin to help lift it, transfer the pastry to line the pie dish. Gently press it in so that it fits snugly. Brush the inside of the pastry with some of the beaten egg to prevent it from becoming soggy.

To make the filling, peel and core the pears and cut into chunks. Place in a bowl and toss together with the lemon juice to prevent the pears from discolouring. Add the cranberries, cinnamon, sugar, flour and salt and toss together with your hands so everything is well mixed. Place the fruit mixture into the pastry case and dot the top of the fruit with the cubes of butter.

Brush the outer edge of the lower pastry case with a little of the beaten egg. Roll out the remaining pastry into a circle just larger than the size of your pie dish and place over the apples. Crimp the pastry by pinching between your fingers. Trim away any excess pastry. You can re-roll this and cut out snowflakes and stars to decorate the top of your pie, if you wish. Cut a slit in the centre of the pie to let any steam escape. Brush the top of the pie and the pastry decorations with a little more egg and sprinkle with sugar.

Bake in the preheated oven for 25 minutes, then reduce the temperature to 170°C (340°F) Gas 3 and bake for about 35 minutes more, until the pastry is golden brown and the fruit is soft. Remove from the oven and let cool for about 15 minutes, then serve straight away with custard or cream, as you prefer.

Pear tart

PÂTE SABLÉE

200 g/1½ cups plain/
all-purpose flour

50 g/½ cup ground almonds

75 g/⅓ cup caster/granulated
sugar

160 g/1½ sticks salted butter,
at room temperature, cubed

1 egg yolk

TART FILLING

65 g/½ stick salted butter,
softened

75 g/⅓ cup caster/
granulated sugar

2 eggs

125 g/1¼ cups ground
almonds

4 large pears, halved
lengthways

apricot jam/jelly, to glaze
(optional)

23-cm/9-inch loose-based
fluted tart pan

SERVES 8–10

Not just a great looking dish, this dessert has it all – buttery pastry, warm frangipane filling and soft fruit. It works with most types of pear, though Comice are particularly good. It can be eaten cold but is hard to beat served warm with cream.

Combine the flour, ground almonds and sugar in a mixing bowl and stir together. Use your fingertips to rub the butter into the mixture until it resembles fine breadcrumbs. Mix the egg yolk in with your hands and knead lightly until the dough comes together into a tight, smooth ball. Wrap the dough in clingfilm/plastic wrap and chill in the refrigerator for 30 minutes until firm. Before using, allow to stand at room temperature for 10–15 minutes.

Preheat the oven to 170°C (340°F) Gas 3.

Roll out the chilled pastry on a lightly floured surface to form a circle about 30 cm/12 inches in diameter and about 3 mm/⅛ inch thick. Drape the pastry over the rolling pin and carefully transfer it to the tart pan. Gently press the pastry into the base so that it fits snugly. The pastry is fragile to handle but any gaps can be repaired using surplus pastry. Trim the top edge with a sharp knife.

To make the frangipane, put the butter and sugar in a large bowl and cream together to a light texture. Beat in the eggs one at a time until the mixture is thoroughly blended. Add the ground almonds and fold in until smooth and even in texture. Spoon into the tart case and spread level with a palette knife.

Using a melon baller or teaspoon, scoop the pips out of the pear halves and discard. Arrange the pears in a circle on top of the frangipane, curved side up. Bake in the preheated oven for about 1 hour or until the frangipane springs back when touched. Remove from the oven and allow to cool.

Boil a little apricot jam/jelly and brush it over the tart to glaze. The tart is best eaten on the day of baking.

Double cranberry and orange pie

AMERICAN PIE CRUST

375 g/3 cups plain/
all-purpose flour

pinch of salt

250 g/1 cup plus 2 tablespoons
cold white cooking fat/
shortening, diced

1 egg, beaten

1 tablespoon white wine
vinegar

4 tablespoons iced water

PIE FILLING

300 g/3 cups fresh or
unthawed frozen cranberries

100 g/3/4 cup dried cranberries

100 g/1/2 cup caster/superfine
sugar, plus extra for sprinkling

3 tablespoons golden syrup/
light corn syrup

finely grated zest and freshly
squeezed juice of 1 tangerine

3 tablespoons orange liqueur

30 g/2 tablespoons unsalted
butter

milk, for brushing

*23-cm/9-inch shallow metal
pie dish*

*baking sheet lined with
baking parchment*

SERVES 6–8

This is the sort of pie you see in Western films, sitting enticingly on the window ledge on a gingham cloth. Both fresh and dried cranberries are used to add texture here.

To make the pastry, sift the flour and salt into a mixing bowl and cut in the fat with a round-bladed knife until well combined. In a separate bowl, mix together the beaten egg, vinegar and water. Pour this mixture into the dry mixture and stir in with the knife. Knead gently on a lightly floured surface until smooth. Wrap in clingfilm/plastic wrap and refrigerate for at least 30 minutes.

Cut the pastry into two pieces, one slightly larger than the other. Roll out the larger piece to a circle just larger than the pie dish. Using your rolling pin to help lift it, transfer the pastry to line the pie dish. Gently press it in so that it fits snugly. Roll out the smaller piece of pastry to a rectangle measuring about 25 x 8 cm/10 x 3 inches. Slip the pastry rectangle onto the prepared baking sheet and cut eight strips. Refrigerate both for 30 minutes.

Preheat oven to 220°C (425°F) Gas 7.

Combine the fresh and dried cranberries in a mixing bowl, add the sugar, syrup, tangerine zest and juice and orange liqueur and mix well. Tip the mixture into the chilled pie crust and dot with the butter. Dampen the rim of the pastry and arrange the lattice strips across the pie in a star shape, pressing down the ends firmly to seal. Trim off the excess pastry and crimp the edges. Brush the pastry with milk and sprinkle heavily with more sugar.

Set the pie on a baking sheet and bake in the preheated oven for 15 minutes. Reduce the oven temperature to 180°C (350°F) Gas 4 and bake for a further 30–40 minutes until the pastry is golden.

Rioja allspice pear and blackberry galette

This is a gorgeous dessert. The dark, moody colours of the pears and blackberries make it outstandingly beautiful and it is just so easy to make. Try serving it warm with salted caramel ice cream – heaven!

PIE CRUST

500 g/18 oz. ready-made puff pastry

1 egg, beaten

demerara/turbinado sugar, for sprinkling

PIE FILLING

750 ml/3 cups Rioja wine

200 g/1 cup brown sugar

1 tablespoon ground allspice

grated zest of 1 orange

8 firm pears, cored and cut into quarters

225 g/1¾ cups fresh blackberries

baking sheet lined with baking parchment

SERVES 6–8

To make the pie filling, pour the rioja wine into a saucepan and add the sugar, allspice and orange zest. Bring to the boil over a medium-high heat. Reduce the heat and simmer for 10 minutes, stirring occasionally, until the sugar has dissolved. Add the pears to the pan and gently cook for 5 minutes.

Preheat the oven to 245°C (475°F) Gas 9, or its highest setting.

Drain the pears into a bowl and reserve the rioja syrup. Cut the pears into thin wedges and set aside.

Pour the wine syrup into a small pan and cook over a medium–high heat until it reduces and thickens. Remove from the heat and set aside.

Roll out the pastry on a lightly floured surface into a rectangle approximately 30 x 15 cm/12 x 6 inches and place on the prepared baking sheet. Arrange the pear slices and blackberries on top leaving a 5-cm/2-inch border all the way round. Fold the edges in and over the fruit, and brush the pastry with the beaten egg. Sprinkle generously with sugar.

Bake in the preheated oven for 15–20 minutes until the pastry is brown and crisp. Serve warm with the rioja syrup poured over.

Strudels, slumps and more

Vanilla and apple strudel

PASTRY

100 g/³/₄ cup plain/
  all-purpose flour

25 ml/1 tablespoon plus
  2 teaspoons warm water

3 tablespoons vegetable oil
  (or use 150 g/5 oz. ready-
  made filo/phyllo pastry)

FILLING

75 g/³/₄ stick
  unsalted butter

50 g/²/₃ cup white or
  wholemeal/whole-wheat
  breadcrumbs

500 g/18 oz. apples, such
  as Granny Smith, Bramley
  or a mixture

grated zest of 1 lemon

1 teaspoon vanilla extract

50 g/¹/₄ cup demerara/
  turbinado sugar

¹/₂ teaspoon ground cinnamon

¹/₂ teaspoon grated nutmeg

50 g/¹/₃ cup (Zante) currants
  (soaked in 1 tablespoon
  brandy, optional)

50 g/¹/₃ cup chopped almonds

1 tablespoon icing/
  confectioners' sugar

SERVES 6–8

Wonderfully retro, strudels are eternally popular, and this vanilla-apple infused specimen will be no exception. Try making the delicate pastry from scratch if you have time, but the ready-made variety gives great results too.

To make the strudel pastry, sift the flour into a bowl. Combine the warm water and oil and stir into the flour until you have a pliable, but not sticky, dough. Knead, then shape into a sausage. Taking one end of the sausage at a time, bash the dough onto a lightly floured work surface until small bubbles appear under the surface. This can take about 15 minutes. Knead it back into a ball and set aside, covered with clingfilm/plastic wrap, for 30 minutes.

Preheat the oven to 200°C (400°F) Gas 6.

To make the filling, heat the butter in a saucepan and gently fry the breadcrumbs until crisp. Peel and coarsely grate the apples, then add the lemon zest, vanilla extract, sugar, cinnamon, nutmeg, currants and almonds.

Roll the dough out on a lightly floured surface and shape into a rectangle. Brush it with the remaining oil. Stretch the dough to a paper-thin consistency by placing the knuckles of your hands underneath it and stretching it out. Alternatively, lay out the filo/phyllo pastry in a large rectangle, approximately 30 x 10 cm/12 x 8 inches.

Spread the apple and currant mixture over your pastry. Roll up the pastry with the contents, making sure to brush and seal both ends and the side with water. Brush the top with melted butter.

Bake in the preheated oven for 30 minutes, or until the pastry is crisp and golden. Sprinkle with icing/confectioners' sugar and serve hot or cold.

Individual pear strudels

When made this way with little oil and no refined sugar, these individual strudels, packed with fruit and aromatic citrus juice, can be a surprisingly healthy vegan option for dessert, breakfast or even lunch boxes.

500 g/18 oz. or 10 large sheets of ready-made filo/phyllo pastry

125 g/15 dried apricots, chopped

2 tablespoons rum

2 teaspoons vanilla extract

freshly squeezed juice and grated zest of 2 lemons or oranges

pinch of salt

8 ripe pears

85 g/1/3 cup apple juice concentrate or pure maple syrup

65 g/1/4 cup coconut oil mixed with 4 tablespoons water

large baking pan, lightly greased

MAKES 20 SLICES

Take the filo/phyllo sheets out of the fridge 30 minutes before making the strudel. This will prevent the sheets from cracking during baking.

Meanwhile, put the apricots in a bowl with the rum, vanilla extract, lemon juice and zest and allow to soak while you prepare the pears, or longer if possible.

Preheat the oven to 180°C (350°F) Gas 4.

Peel and core the pears. Cut them into small cubes and mix them with the soaked apricots and the apple concentrate or syrup. Divide the mixture into 5 equal portions.

Place a sheet of filo/phyllo on a dry work surface with the longer side facing you. (Cover the remaining sheets with clingfilm/plastic wrap to prevent them from drying out.) Brush the coconut oil mixture lightly over the sheet. Cover it with another sheet (this one doesn't need oiling).

Spread one portion of pears lengthwise along the bottom edge of the sheet. Arrange them in a 6-cm/2½-inch-wide strip, leaving a 2-cm/¾-inch edge on each side to prevent the filling from spilling out. Roll the sheet up carefully around the filling and place in the baking pan. Repeat with the remaining sheets and filling to get 5 strudels in the pan. Brush them lightly with the coconut oil mixture and use a sharp knife to score each strudel into 4 slices.

Bake the strudels in the preheated oven for 25–30 minutes or until golden. Serve warm or cold.

Cherry and ricotta strudel

Here, fresh ricotta cheese is combined with summer-ripe cherries and crisp filo/phyllo pastry to great effect. Best of all, you can make this strudel in advance and freeze it before baking. There is no need to thaw before cooking – just give it a little more time in the oven until it's hot all the way through.

500 g/18 oz.
  fresh cherries, pitted

60 g/½ cup icing/
  confectioners' sugar,
  plus extra for dusting

2 teaspoons cornflour/
  cornstarch

100 g/1 cup ground almonds

150 g/⅔ cup ricotta cheese

8 sheets of filo/phyllo pastry,
  thawed if frozen

75 g/¾ stick unsalted butter,
  melted

SERVES 8

Put the cherries, 1 tablespoon of the icing/confectioners' sugar and the cornflour/cornstarch in a bowl and let sit for 30 minutes, stirring often.

Preheat the oven to 220°C (425°F) Gas 7.

Put the ground almonds and 2 tablespoons of the icing/confectioners' sugar in a bowl and mix to combine. Put the ricotta in a separate bowl, add the remaining icing/confectioners' sugar and mix to combine. Set aside until needed. Put a baking sheet in the preheated oven to heat up. (This will prevent the bottom of the filo/phyllo from becoming soggy.)

Put a sheet of baking parchment on a work surface. Lay a sheet of filo/phyllo pastry on the baking parchment, with the longest edge nearest to you. Brush all over with melted butter and sprinkle all over with 1–2 tablespoons of the ground almond mixture. Repeat with the remaining sheets of pastry and the butter and almond mixture, finishing with the final sheet of pastry.

Working quickly so that the pastry does not get soggy, spread the ricotta mixture over the pastry, leaving a 5-cm/2-inch margin around the edges. Spoon the cherry mixture over the top. Fold the edge nearest to you up and over the filling, tucking in the shorter edges as you roll. Make sure the strudel is sitting seam-side down. Use the baking paper to lift the strudel onto the hot baking sheet. Bake in the preheated oven for 12–15 minutes until the pastry is golden. Leave to cool slightly before dusting liberally with icing/confectioners' sugar and cutting into slices to serve.

Apricot and almond slump

The word 'slump' perfectly describes the batter that surrounds the seasonal fruit in this satisfying pudding. Normally the fruit is on the bottom and the thick batter spooned or poured roughly over the top but if you like to see more fruit, pour the batter in first, then push in the fruit. You can use any juicy fruits, and berries are really good too.

600 g/1¼ lb. fresh apricots

150 g/¾ cup golden caster/natural cane sugar

30 g/¼ cup whole blanched almonds

SLUMP BATTER

200 g/1½ cups plain/all-purpose flour

3 teaspoons baking powder

pinch of salt

100 g/1 cup ground almonds

about 350 ml/1½ cups whole milk

4 tablespoons unsalted butter, melted

vanilla ice cream, to serve (optional)

large non-stick baking pan, greased

SERVES 4–6

Preheat the oven to 190°C (375°F) Gas 5.

Halve the apricots, remove the pits and mix with 100 g/½ cup of the sugar. Set aside until needed.

Sift the flour, baking powder, salt and remaining sugar into a bowl. Stir in the ground almonds, the milk and melted butter and whisk until smooth and thick. Pour the batter into the prepared pan, then push in the apricots cut-side up but in a higgledy-piggledy manner and slightly at an angle all over. Place a whole almond inside each apricot where the pit once was.

Bake in the preheated oven for 25–30 minutes, until risen and golden. Let cool slightly before serving with vanilla ice cream as you prefer.

- 900 g/2 lb. pears, peeled, cored and sliced
- 75 g/⅓ cup light brown soft sugar
- 2 tablespoons plain/all-purpose flour
- 1 teaspoon vanilla extract
- finely grated zest of 1 orange

SLUMP BATTER

- 300 g/2¼ cups plain/all-purpose flour
- 200 g/1 cup caster/granulated sugar
- 1 tablespoon baking powder
- pinch of salt
- 250 ml/1 cup whole milk
- 125 g/1⅛ sticks unsalted butter, melted
- extra sugar or cinnamon sugar, to sprinkle
- vanilla ice cream or whipped cream, to serve (optional)
- *large, shallow ovenproof dish, well greased*

SERVES 4–6

Pear slump

This is a homely dish, easy to make and a most welcome sight at the dinner table on a cold winter's evening. If you prefer to use apples, choose a tart green variety and replace the grated orange zest with lemon.

Preheat the oven to 190°C (375°F) Gas 5.

In a bowl, combine the pears, sugar, flour, vanilla extract and orange zest. Toss with your hands to combine and arrange in an even layer in the bottom of the prepared ovenproof dish. Set aside.

To prepare the slump batter, combine the flour, sugar, baking powder and salt in a separate bowl. In a third bowl or jug/pitcher, stir together the milk and melted butter. Gradually pour the milk mixture into the dry ingredients, beating with a wooden spoon until just smooth.

Drop spoonfuls of the batter on top of the pears, leaving gaps but spreading to the edges. Sprinkle the top with sugar and bake in the preheated oven for 40–50 minutes, until golden brown. Serve warm with vanilla ice cream or whipped cream, as preferred.

Germknödel

A traditional Austrian treat, the germknödel is a cross between a doughnut and a steamed bun. The beautifully plump buns are filled with a sharp plum jam/jelly and served doused in a creamy vanilla sauce.

500 g/3½ cups strong white bread flour

1 teaspoon fine sea salt

3 tablespoons caster/superfine sugar

30 g/1 oz. fresh yeast (or 2 × 7-g/¼-oz. sachets dried yeast)

250 ml/generous 1 cup whole milk, warmed

35 g/¼ stick plus 1 teaspoon unsalted butter, melted and cooled, plus extra melted butter, to brush

2 eggs, beaten

10 generous teaspoons plum jam/jelly

poppy seeds, to serve

VANILLA SAUCE

500 ml/2 cups whole milk

2 tablespoons cornflour/cornstarch

2 egg yolks

200 g/1 cup caster/superfine sugar

2 tablespoons vanilla extract

60 g/½ stick unsalted butter, melted

baking sheet, lightly greased

SERVES 10

Mix the flour with the salt and sugar in a large bowl. Mix the yeast with 2 tablespoons of the warm milk and leave to stand for a few minutes until frothy. Add this, along with the rest of the milk, the melted butter and the eggs, to the flour. Mix to form a dough.

Turn out onto a lightly floured surface and knead vigorously for 10 minutes. Put back into the bowl and cover with a clean kitchen cloth. Leave to rise in a warm place for about 1 hour or until doubled in size.

Knock back the dough, then divide into 10 pieces. Flatten each piece out on the work surface, then dollop a spoonful of the jam/jelly into the centre. Bring the dough around the jam/jelly and seal well by pinching the edges together with your fingers.

Place on the prepared baking sheet and cover with the kitchen cloth. Leave for 30–60 minutes until doubled in size.

Meanwhile, to make the vanilla sauce, heat the milk in a saucepan until almost boiling. Whisk the cornflour/cornstarch, egg yolks, sugar and vanilla together in a bowl, then pour over the hot milk. Return to the pan over a low heat. Cook, stirring, until thick. Add the melted butter and keep warm while you steam the buns.

Bring a very large saucepan of water to the boil – you can use a bamboo steamer or a normal steamer lined with baking parchment, otherwise you can use the traditional Austrian method: brush a clean cotton kitchen cloth with melted butter and put over the saucepan, then secure in place with twine, making sure no cloth is exposed to the heat source. Put the dumplings, a few at a time, on top of the steamer. Cover with the steamer lid or a second large pan. Steam for 15 minutes.

Brush with a little melted butter and scatter with poppy seeds. Serve the dumplings smothered in the vanilla sauce.

Apple brown betty

7 slices stale brown bread

8 apples (Bramley, Granny Smith and Pink Lady are all good choices), cored, sliced and diced

freshly squeezed juice of 1 lemon

125 g/²/₃ cup light muscovado sugar

2 teaspoons ground cinnamon

2 teaspoons pure vanilla extract

75 g/³/₄ stick unsalted butter, melted

cream or vanilla ice cream, to serve (optional)

baking dish, greased

SERVES 8–10

A brown betty is a traditional American dessert, with similarities to the British crumble (see pages 10-29). The perfect way to use up seasonal fruit and stale breadcrumbs, the brown betty is old-fashioned comfort food at its best.

Preheat the oven to 180°C (350°F) Gas 4.

Blitz the slices of bread in a food processor to make crumbs.

In a large bowl, toss the apples with the lemon juice, then scatter half in the base of the prepared dish. In a separate bowl, mix the breadcrumbs with the sugar, cinnamon, vanilla and melted butter. Sprinkle half of the breadcrumb mixture over the layer of apples. Scatter over the remaining apples and top the dessert with the remaining breadcrumbs.

Bake in the preheated oven for 35–40 minutes, or until the apples are soft. If the breadcrumbs brown too quickly, you can cover the top with a sheet of foil. Serve warm with cream or vanilla ice cream, as preferred.

Buttered apricot betty

Sometimes simple things are the best, and this gorgeous dessert is one that can be made with very few ingredients and a small amount of effort. The smell of the sweet apricots as it bakes will have your mouth watering!

675 g/1½ lb. fresh apricots or 3 x 400-g/14-oz. cans apricots in juice (not syrup)

100 g/1 stick minus 1 tablespoon unsalted butter, cubed

150 g/2¾ cups fresh breadcrumbs, lightly toasted

2 tablespoons golden/corn syrup

100 ml/⅓ cup fresh orange juice

50 g/3½ tablespoons caster/granulated sugar

cream, to serve (optional)

medium deep pie or soufflé dish, greased

SERVES 4

Preheat the oven to 190°C (375°F) Gas 5.

Cut the fresh apricots in half and remove the pits (or drain the canned apricots and pat dry). Arrange a thin layer of apricots in the bottom of the prepared dish.

Reserving 4–6 tablespoons of breadcrumbs for the top, sprinkle some of the rest of the breadcrumbs over the apricots in the baking dish and dot with some of the butter. Put in another layer of apricots and repeat these alternate layers until all the apricots and breadcrumbs are used. Top with the reserved breadcrumbs.

Warm the syrup with the orange juice, and pour this evenly over the top. Sprinkle with the sugar and dot with the remaining butter.

Place the dish in a roasting pan and pour in enough boiling water to come halfway up the sides of the dish. Bake in the preheated oven for 45 minutes, until the apricots are soft and the top is crisp and browned. Serve warm with cream, if you like.

Pineapple and rum betty with coconut

Pineapple, rum and coconut – three flavours that are just made for each other. Blocks of creamed coconut are perfect for grating into desserts, as you can use just the amount you like, and the rest keeps for a long while in a plastic bag.

1 medium pineapple

75 g/1 cup unsweetened desiccated/dried coconut

75 g/2³/₄ oz. Madeira cake or similar, blitzed into crumbs in a food processor

75-g/2³/₄-oz. piece of creamed coconut block, grated

75 g/³/₄ stick unsalted butter

100 g/3¹/₂ oz. macadamia nuts, roughly chopped

2 tablespoons golden/corn syrup

100 ml/¹/₃ cup dark or golden rum

cream, to serve (optional)

deep pie dish or soufflé dish, greased

SERVES 6

Preheat the oven to 190°C (375°F) Gas 5.

Cut the top and bottom off the pineapple, then cut off the skin, removing the 'eyes' using the tip of a potato peeler. Cut into quarters and then take out the hard core. Slice thinly.

Spread the desiccated/dried coconut evenly over a baking sheet and toast in the preheated oven for about 5 minutes, until pale golden brown. Mix with the crumbed cake and half of the grated creamed coconut.

Place a layer of the sliced pineapple in the prepared baking dish. Reserve 4–6 tablespoons of the toasted coconut mixture for the top. Sprinkle some of the rest of the coconut mix over the pineapple and dot with some of the butter. Put in some more pineapple and repeat these alternate layers until all the pineapple and coconut are used up. Mix the reserved coconut with the chopped macadamia nuts and use this for the final top layer.

In a small saucepan, warm the golden/corn syrup with the rum and pour this over the top. Sprinkle with the remaining grated creamed coconut and dot with the remaining butter. Place the pie dish in a roasting pan and pour in enough boiling water to come half way up the sides of the dish. Bake in the preheated oven for 35–40 minutes, until the pineapple is soft and the top crisp and brown. If the top browns too much, lay a piece of foil loosely on top. Serve warm with cream, or as desired.

Cherry clafoutis

This irresistible French dessert marries ripe berries with a light, sweet batter. Cherries are the most traditional choice for clafoutis, but blueberries and raspberries are great alternatives. Purists believe the cherries should not be pitted before baking, citing extra flavour as an excuse. However, if you value your teeth more than tradition, make yours like this one without the pits!

450 g/1 lb. ripe fresh cherries, pitted

2 tablespoons caster/granulated sugar

3–4 tablespoons Kirsch or brandy

CLAFOUTIS BATTER

75 g/⅓ cup caster/granulated sugar

2 eggs

50 g/⅓ cup plus 1 tablespoon plain/all-purpose flour

125 ml/½ cup whole milk

2 teaspoons pure vanilla extract

25 g/2 tablespoons unsalted butter, melted

pinch of salt

1 tablespoon caster/superfine sugar, for sprinkling

cream, to serve (optional)

20-cm/8-inch pie dish, well greased

SERVES 6–8

Preheat the oven to 180°C (350°F) Gas 4.

Stir together the cherries, sugar and Kirsch (or brandy) in a bowl and leave to macerate for a few hours, or even overnight.

To make the batter, whisk together the sugar and eggs in a large mixing bowl. Sift over the flour and whisk until fully incorporated. Slowly whisk in the milk, followed by the vanilla and melted butter. Stir in the salt and tip the cherries and their juices into the batter.

Pour into the prepared pie dish and bake in the preheated oven for 35–45 minutes, or until a skewer inserted comes out clean. Sprinkle with the caster/superfine sugar and serve warm, preferably with a generous pouring of chilled cream.

Pear and fig clafoutis *with almonds*

3 ripe pears

3 ripe figs

CLAFOUTIS BATTER

200 ml/¾ cup crème fraîche

200 ml/generous ¾ cup
   whole milk

3 eggs

125 g/⅔ cup minus
   2 teaspoons caster/
   granulated sugar

2 tablespoons ground almonds

½ teaspoon ground cinnamon

icing/confectioners' sugar,
   to dust

cream, to serve (optional)

baking dish, well greased

SERVES 4–6

This delicious dessert is ideal for entertaining because it looks attractive, with the beautiful colours of the fresh figs, yet is so easy to prepare. Simply make the batter and prepare the fruit in advance, then combine the two and bake at the start of the meal. It will be done by the time you are ready to serve.

Preheat the oven to 200°C (400°F) Gas 6.

Peel and core the pears and cut into medium-large pieces. Trim the stem ends from the figs and cut into slightly smaller pieces. If there is too much white on the skins, trim this off. Put the fruit in the prepared baking dish and distribute evenly. Set aside.

In a mixing bowl, combine the crème fraîche, milk, eggs, sugar, almonds and cinnamon. Mix well with a hand-held electric whisk.

Pour the batter evenly over the fruit and bake in the preheated oven until puffed and golden, about 35–45 minutes. Let cool slightly and dust with icing/confectioners' sugar just before serving. Serve warm with cream, if you like.

Puddings and dessert cakes

Spiced apple and croissant bake with Calvados

What to do with leftover slightly stale croissants? Make this spiced apple and croissant bake, of course! The French have something resembling this recipe which is made with fried stale bread and a custard sauce (wonderfully entitled 'pain perdu', ie. 'lost bread') but that is closer to French toast. This boozy, spiced pudding is rich and indulgent, ideal if you are looking for something a bit different from basic apple pie!

500 ml/2 cups whole milk

500 ml/2 cups double/
heavy cream

1 vanilla pod/bean, split

1 cinnamon stick

3 star anise

2 tablespoons Calvados

3 eggs

3 egg yolks

200 g/1 cup caster/
granulated sugar

2 croissants, slightly stale

2 tablespoons unsalted butter,
melted

2 Braeburn apples or similar
sweet yet tart eating apples

2 tablespoons semi-dried
apples, chopped

whipped cream mixed with a
little lemon zest and vanilla
extract, to serve (optional)

*large pie dish or baking pan,
well greased*

SERVES 4–6

Preheat the oven to 200°C (400°F) Gas 6.

Put the milk, cream, vanilla, cinnamon, star anise and Calvados in a saucepan over a medium heat and bring just to the boil.

Meanwhile, put the whole eggs, egg yolks and sugar in a stand mixer or use a hand-held electric whisk to beat together until pale and fluffy. Slowly pour the boiled cream into the egg mixture, while whisking vigorously, until evenly incorporated.

Pass the mixture through a fine sieve/strainer and discard the vanilla pod/bean, cinnamon stick and star anise.

Cut the croissants in half horizontally and brush the melted butter over them. Arrange them in the prepared pie dish or baking pan.

Halve, core and roughly chop the fresh apples. Scatter these and the semi-dried apples over the croissants in the pan, then pour the custard in over the top. Using a spatula, press down the croissants so that they soak up some of the custard mixture.

Bake in the preheated oven for 25 minutes. The custard should still be a little runny in the middle. Serve with whipped cream flavoured with a little lemon and vanilla extract, if desired.

Raspberry croissant puddings

These little puddings would be at home both on the breakfast table served with Greek-style yogurt and at the close of an evening meal served with puddles of ice cream or cream. The croissants transform an English-style bread pudding into a French-style dessert, yet you could easily substitute leftover brioche, panettone or a loaf of whatever you have to hand.

2 eggs

3 egg yolks

1 teaspoon vanilla extract

475 ml/2 cups whole milk

100 g/½ cup caster/
granulated sugar

6 croissants, slightly stale

150 g/1 cup raspberries
(if frozen, let them defrost
and strain the juices), plus
a few extra to serve

6 ramekins, greased

SERVES 6

Preheat the oven to 180°C (350°F) Gas 4.

Whisk the eggs, egg yolks, vanilla, milk and sugar together in a bowl. Tear the croissants into pieces the size of a matchbook. Place half the croissants across the bottom of the ramekins. Add the raspberries, then the remaining croissant pieces.

Pour the custard over the croissants and allow to soak for 10 minutes. Cover each ramekin with foil and puncture the top to let the steam escape. Try not to let the foil touch the mixture.

Put the ramekins in a deep baking pan. Pour hot water into the pan until it comes halfway up the sides of the ramekins. Bake in the preheated oven for 40 minutes or until the custard is set. Serve warm with extra fresh raspberries.

Bread and butter pudding with grilled peaches

4 ripe peaches

6 slices of gluten-free bread (the crustier, the better)

2–3 tablespoons coconut oil or non-hydrogenated sunflower spread

large handful of raisins and/ or sultanas/golden raisins

500 ml/2 cups coconut milk (try not to substitute this for another non-dairy milk, as the thicker coconut milk stands in for double/heavy cream here)

3 tablespoons xylitol or stevia (xylitol works best here)

1½ tablespoons cornflour/ cornstarch

1 teaspoon ground cinnamon

6 ramekins

SERVES 6

This gluten-and dairy-free version of the comforting classic bread and butter pudding includes sweet and sticky caramelized peaches, which work really well. Cooking and serving these in their individual ramekins means that you can eat them straight from the dish, no extra washing up required!

Preheat the grill/broiler to medium.

Remove the pits from the peaches, then cut the flesh into cubes. Place them in an ovenproof dish and grill/broil for about 3 minutes until they start to caramelize.

Remove the peaches from the grill/broiler, and preheat the oven to 180°C (350°F) Gas 4.

Toast the slices of bread, then spread the coconut oil or sunflower spread over both sides of each slice. Cut the toast into cubes about 2 cm/1 inch wide. Mix with the peaches and dried fruit, then divide the mixture equally between the ramekins.

Put the coconut milk and sweetener in a saucepan over a medium heat and leave until warm. Stir in the cornflour/cornstarch and you will see the mixture start to thicken. Remove the pan from the heat and allow the mixture to cool until it is lukewarm. Stir in the cinnamon, then pour the mixture equally into the ramekins.

Bake the puddings in the preheated oven for about 25–30 minutes until firm. They are best served freshly baked, but they can also be reheated for 4–5 minutes the day after baking.

Apricot frangipane puddings

All you really need for a good frangipane is butter, sugar, eggs and ground almonds, though a small amount of flour helps give these upside-down puddings a bit more structural integrity. The hot puddings are delicious topped with a scoop of ice cream, which will melt like pooling snow over the pudding's craggy tops.

450 g/1 lb. apricot flesh (about 10 pitted fresh apricots)

50 g/¼ cup brown/muscovado sugar

110 g/1 stick unsalted butter, at room temperature

110 g/½ cup caster/granulated sugar

2 UK large/US extra-large eggs, beaten

130 g/1⅓ cup ground almonds

3 tablespoons plain/all-purpose flour, plus extra for dusting

icing/confectioners' sugar, for dusting

ice cream, to serve (optional)

6 ramekins, greased and dusted with flour

SERVES 6

Preheat the oven to 180°C (350°F) Gas 4.

Cut the apricots into quarters and simmer in a pan with the brown sugar and 1 tablespoon water for 3 minutes. Arrange the apricots over the bottom of the ramekins.

Cream the butter and caster/granulated sugar together until pale and fluffy, then beat in the eggs one at a time. Carefully fold in the almonds and flour, then spoon the mixture over the apricots.

Bake in the preheated oven for 30 minutes. Remove from the oven and leave to cool for 5 minutes, then turn out onto serving plates, ensuring all of the fruit tumbles out to sit on top of the frangipane.

Dust with icing/confectioners' sugar and serve with ice cream, if you like.

Queen of puddings

600 ml/2½ cups whole milk

seeds of 1 vanilla pod/bean

finely grated zest of 1 lemon

25 g/2 tablespoons unsalted butter

50 g/¼ cup caster/granulated sugar

3 egg yolks

100 g/1½ cups brioche/challah crumbs

6 tablespoons raspberry jam/jelly

vanilla ice cream, to serve (optional)

MERINGUE TOP

3 egg whites

pinch of salt

170 g/¾ cup caster/superfine sugar

1 teaspoon cornflour/cornstarch

½ teaspoon white wine vinegar

2 teaspoons pure vanilla extract

vanilla ice cream, to serve (optional)

large oval pie dish, greased

piping/pastry bag fitted with a star-shaped nozzle/tip (optional)

SERVES 6–8

With a base made from soaked breadcrumbs covered in jam/jelly and then topped with meringue, this old fashioned British pudding has similarities to Monmouth pudding and Manchester pudding. It has been said that Queen Victoria enjoyed a portion of Manchester pudding on a royal visit and so the dish was renamed, 'Queen of Puddings', in her honour. Whatever the origins of the name, this delicious dessert is certainly worthy of royalty.

Preheat the oven to 170°C (340°F) Gas 3.

To make the base, put the milk, vanilla, lemon zest and butter in a saucepan over a gentle heat to warm. Meanwhile, whisk the sugar with the egg yolks in a large mixing bowl. When the milk is hot, but not boiling, whisk it into the egg yolks. Add the brioche/challah crumbs to the custard and leave to soak for 15–20 minutes, to allow the crumbs to swell.

Pour the mixture into the prepared dish and bake in the preheated oven for 30–35 minutes or until set. Remove it from the oven and spread the jam/jelly evenly over the top.

Reduce the oven temperature to 150°C (300°F) Gas 2.

In a large mixing bowl, whisk the egg whites with the salt until stiff. Gradually add the sugar, continuing to whisk in between each addition until you have a thick, glossy meringue. Whisk in the cornflour/cornstarch, vinegar and vanilla.

You can either pile the meringue on top of the jam/jelly and swirl it with a fork, or you can pipe it using a star-shaped nozzle/tip. Bake in the preheated oven for 20–25 minutes, or until the meringue is firm and slightly golden. Serve hot with vanilla ice cream, if you like.

Layered plum crunch dessert

This magnificent dessert features layers of mascarpone cream, roasted cinnamon plums and buttery crumbly crunch – just perfect for digging in with a big spoon!

ROASTED PLUMS

1.2 kg/2¾ lbs. ripe red plums

100 g/½ cup caster/ granulated sugar

1 teaspoon ground cinnamon

1 teaspoon pure vanilla extract or ½ teaspoon vanilla pod/ bean powder

CRUNCH LAYER

200 g/1¾ sticks unsalted butter

300 g/2¼ cups self-raising/ self-rising flour

150 g/¾ cup caster/ granulated sugar

CREAM LAYER

500 ml/2 cups mascarpone

600 ml/2½ cups double/ heavy cream

3 tablespoons icing/ confectioners' sugar, sifted

large baking sheet, lined with baking parchment

large glass dish

SERVES 10

Preheat the oven to 180°C (350°F) Gas 4.

Cut the plums in half and remove the pits. Put the plums in a roasting pan and sprinkle with the sugar, cinnamon and vanilla and pour over 125 ml/½ cup of water. Bake in the preheated oven for 30–40 minutes, depending on the ripeness of the plums, until soft. Leave the plums to cool but keep the oven on.

Prepare the crunch layer while the plums are cooking. In a large mixing bowl, rub the butter into the flour using your fingertips until the mixture resembles fine breadcrumbs and comes together when you press it. Mix in the sugar. Spread out on the prepared baking sheet and bake in the preheated oven for 10–15 minutes until golden brown, stirring halfway through to ensure that the crumble does not burn. Pour into a dish and leave to cool.

When the crunch and plums are completely cool, whisk together the mascarpone, double/heavy cream and icing/confectioners' sugar until thick.

To assemble, sprinkle one-quarter of the crunch mixture over the base of the glass dish. Top with one-third of the plums and spread out evenly. Cover with one-third of the cream mixture and spread out in an even layer. Repeat for two more layers, ending with an extra layer of crunch on top. Chill in the refrigerator for 3 hours before serving.

Soda pop dump cake

The basic recipe for a dump cake is simple: dump all of the ingredients into a cake pan and let the oven work its magic. The key ingredients for dump cakes are a box of cake mix and a can of soda pop (in this case Sprite), which helps it to rise. This is possibly the easiest cake you will ever make!

300 g/2½ cups fresh blueberries

150 g/½ cup blueberry jam/jelly, plus extra to serve

1 box vanilla cake mix

1 can clear, sparkling lemonade, such as Sprite

whipped cream, to serve

30 x 18 x 4-cm/11 x 7 x 1½-inch cake pan

SERVES 12

Preheat the oven to 180°C (350°F) Gas 4.

Empty the blueberries into the bottom of the cake pan (no need to grease the pan). Dollop spoonfuls of jam/jelly over the blueberries.

In a separate bowl, whisk together the cake mix and lemonade. It will foam and still be a bit lumpy, but that is normal.

Pour the cake batter over the blueberries and jam/jelly and make sure it covers the whole pan. Don't worry if some of the jam/jelly leaks into the batter – that adds deliciousness!

Bake in the preheated oven for 30–40 minutes until the top of the cake is golden brown and it is springy to the touch.

Serve immediately with whipped cream and more blueberry jam/jelly on top. This cake is best eaten warm on the day it is made.

TIP You could melt the blueberry jam/jelly in a saucepan over low heat to drizzle over the top but dolloping more on top of warm cake will work just as well.

Boozy berry mug cake

Fruit preserves swirled into a soft brandy-topped sponge makes the most warming, comforting and sweet mug cake. It is literally a hug in a mug!

2 tablespoons unsalted butter

1 teaspoon vanilla extract

1 egg

2 tablespoons caster/granulated sugar

5 tablespoons self-raising/rising flour

2 tablespoons raspberry jam/jelly

1 tablespoon brandy

TO SERVE

jam/jelly

whipped cream

fresh fruit

microwavable mug

MAKES 1

Put the butter into the mug and microwave for 20–30 seconds at 800W until melted.

Stir in the vanilla, then use a fork to beat in the egg until fully combined. Add the sugar and stir thoroughly. Pour in the flour and mix thoroughly until you have a thick cake batter.

Temporarily remove a couple of spoonfuls of the mixture into a separate bowl.

Drop the jam/jelly on top of the mixture in the mug and using a fork, gently swirl it in, before pouring the brandy over the top.

Empty the mixture that was in the separate bowl back over the top. (The brandy will still be quite liquid on top, so carefully smooth the batter so that the jam is covered.)

Put the mug on a plate and microwave for 1 minute 50 seconds at 800W. The cake will rise and then sink a little and should still be a little wet to touch. (You should place it on a plate in case any of the jam/jelly leaks.)

Leave the mug cake to cool for 3 minutes before spreading with a little extra jam/jelly and topping with a swirl of whipped cream. You can also choose to adorn yours with fresh raspberries or other fresh fruit to match the flavour of the jam/jelly. Be careful when eating as the jam/jelly centre will still be quite hot.

Roulade with provençal peaches

4 eggs

100 g/½ cup golden caster/
natural cane sugar

2 tablespoons unsalted butter,
melted

½ teaspoon rock salt

125 g/1 cup plain/all-purpose
flour, sifted

icing/confectioners' sugar,
for dusting

225 g/1½ cups fresh
raspberries

crème fraîche, to serve

PROVENÇAL PEACHES

150 g/¾ cup caster/
superfine sugar

400 ml/1⅔ cups oz. rosé wine

1 teaspoon edible lavender
flowers

6 small firm, white peaches,
peeled

13 x 9-inch/33 x 23-cm baking
sheet, lined with baking
parchment and lightly
greased

SERVES 6–8

Update the classic jelly/jam Swiss roll into a ridiculously delicious dessert by adding peaches macerated in rosé wine.

To make the provençal peaches, in a saucepan, bring the sugar and wine to the boil over a medium-high heat. Reduce the heat and simmer for 5 minutes until the sugar has dissolved. Remove from the heat and stir in the lavender flowers. Let cool for 5 minutes, then strain the syrup through a fine-mesh sieve/strainer. Pour the syrup over the peaches, then leave to macerate in the syrup for at least 2 hours or overnight.

Preheat the oven to 190°C (375°F) Gas 5.

Whisk together the eggs and sugar for 5–6 minutes in a stand mixer or using a hand-held electric whisk until pale and fluffy. Pour in the melted butter, add the salt and stir to combine. Slowly fold in the flour, then pour the batter onto the prepared baking sheet. Spread out evenly and bake in the preheated oven for 10–12 minutes until golden and springy.

Remove from the oven and set aside for a few minutes. Sprinkle a clean kitchen cloth with icing/confectioners' sugar. Invert the cake onto the towel and remove the baking parchment from the base. Beginning with the short sides, roll the cake up in the towel and leave to cool for 2 hours.

Drain the peaches from their syrup and reserve both. Slice the peaches and toss with the raspberries in a bowl. Unroll the cake and remove the kitchen cloth. Spread the crème fraîche evenly over the cake. Scatter the sliced peaches and raspberries over the cake, then roll it up tightly. Place the cake seam-side down on a serving platter.

Place the peach syrup in a small saucepan and bring to the boil until reduced by half. Dust the cake with icing/confectioners' sugar and serve with the warm syrup.

600 ml/2½ cups cherry juice

honey, to sweeten (optional)

230 g/½ lb. whole cherries, halved and pitted

50 g/⅓ cup sour/tart cherries, roughly chopped

flaked/slivered almonds, to sprinkle

cocoa powder, to dust (optional)

PASTRY

80 g/⅔ cup arrowroot powder

185 g/generous 1¾ cups almond flour

80 g/5½ tablespoons coconut butter

1 egg

1 beaten egg, for brushing

ALMOND FRANGIPANE

270 g/2¾ cups ground almonds

150 g/generous ½ cup honey

75 ml/⅓ cup hemp milk

3 tablespoons coconut flour

seeds from 1 vanilla pod/bean

2½ teaspoons pure almond extract

3 eggs

30 x 25-cm/12 x 10-inch baking pan, greased and lined with baking parchment

SERVES 8–10

Cherry frangipane traybake

Enjoy a slice of this traybake served warm as a dessert or cold with a selection of other afternoon tea treats.

Pour the cherry juice into a saucepan and simmer over a medium heat until the juice reduces down and is thick and glossy. You can add a little honey if the result is too sharp for your taste. Set aside until ready to serve.

Preheat the oven to 180°C (350°F) Gas 4.

To make the pastry, mix together the arrowroot and flour in a large mixing bowl and rub in the coconut butter with your fingertips until the texture resembles breadcrumbs.

In a separate bowl, beat the egg and 3–4 tablespoons of water together, then add to the flour mixture. Mix together and form into a dough. Roll out between two pieces of baking parchment to the size of the baking pan. Using your rolling pin to help lift it, transfer the pastry to line the pan and gently press it in so that it fits snugly.

Brush the pastry with the beaten egg and bake in the preheated oven for 10 minutes, or until golden. Keep the oven on.

To make the almond frangipane, mix all of the ingredients together. Spread evenly across baked pastry base and top with the halved and sour/tart cherries. Sprinkle with flaked/slivered almonds and bake in the preheated oven for 20–30 minutes until golden.

Drizzle with the reserved sour cherry syrup and dust with cocoa powder, if desired, to serve.

Apricot and orange traybake

Apricots and oranges bring a decidedly summery flavour to this easy-to-make traybake. Fresh apricots are pretty much available all year round these days, but organic dried ones work well too - you just need to remember to soak them overnight in advance so that they are nice and soft.

150 g/1¼ sticks salted butter, softened

200 g/1 cup caster/ granulated sugar

3 eggs, lightly beaten

finely grated zest of 3 oranges

45 g/⅓ cup plain/all-purpose flour

180 g/1½ cups self-raising/ self-rising flour

6 fresh apricots, halved and pitted

1 tablespoon demerara/ turbinado sugar

34 x 20 x 3-cm/14 x 8 x 1-inch baking pan, lined with baking parchment

MAKES 10 SLICES

Preheat the oven to 170°C (340°F) Gas 3.

Cream the butter and sugar together in a large bowl until pale and fluffy. Add the beaten eggs in two stages, stirring to a smooth batter each time. Stir in the orange zest. Sift the flours together, then add to the mixture and stir to a smooth paste.

Spoon the mixture into the prepared baking pan and spread level. Arrange the apricots, cut side up, on the surface of the mixture and sprinkle the sugar evenly over the cake. Bake in the preheated oven for about 40 minutes. A skewer inserted into the middle of the cake should come out clean. Remove from the oven and run a knife around the sides of the pan before turning out onto a wire rack. Serve warm.

Berry and hazelnut crumble cake

You can experiment with using different berries and types of jam/jelly in this cake, which combines the any-time pleasure of a classic sponge cake with the delicious treat of moist fruit and a crumble topping.

150 g/1¼ sticks unsalted butter, softened

175 g/¾ cup plus 2 tablespoons caster/granulated sugar

2 UK large/US extra-large eggs

125 g/1 cup minus 1 tablespoon self-raising/self-rising flour

50 g/⅓ cup polenta/cornmeal

1 teaspoon baking powder

finely grated zest of 1 small lemon

50 g/¼ cup Greek yogurt

175 g/scant ⅔ cup blackcurrant jam/jelly

175 g/6 oz. fresh raspberries

CRUMBLE TOPPING

100 g/¾ cup shelled, blanched whole hazelnuts

75 g/⅓ cup plus 2 teaspoons demerara/turbinado sugar

75 g/¾ stick cold unsalted butter, cubed

100 g/¾ cup self-raising/self-rising flour

23-cm/9-inch loose-based cake pan, lightly greased and lined with baking parchment

SERVES 12

Preheat the oven to 180°C (350°F) Gas 4.

To make the crumble topping, chop the nuts by hand or pulse them in a food processor – you want them to be roughly chopped. Pulse the sugar, butter and flour in a food processor until combined, then add 1–2 tablespoons cold water and briefly whiz again until the mixture resembles breadcrumbs. Mix in the nuts. Alternatively, you can rub the butter into the flour by hand in a mixing bowl, then stir in the sugar, water and nuts. Set aside.

To make the cake, combine the butter, sugar, eggs, flour, polenta/cornmeal, baking powder, lemon zest and yogurt in a mixing bowl and beat with a hand-held electric whisk until combined.

Spoon the mixture into the prepared pan and spread it evenly. Tip the jam/jelly into a bowl and mix it with a spoon to loosen it, then distribute spoonfuls over the top of the cake mixture. Using the tip of a round-bladed knife, gently spread the jam/jelly by lightly swirling it into the top of the cake mixture. Sprinkle a third of the crumble mixture on top, scatter the raspberries over this, then finish with the remaining crumble topping.

Put the cake on a baking sheet and bake in the preheated oven for 1 hour 5 minutes–1 hour 10 minutes, until a skewer inserted into the middle comes out just clean. Leave to cool in the pan before transferring to a serving plate or board to serve.

Index

Credits

PHOTOGRAPHY

Peter Cassidy pp. 6a & bl, 8, 32–35, 39, 40, 45, 47, 55, 76, 84, 86, 87, 92, 95, 99, endpapers

Laura Edwards p.85

Tara Fisher p.12

Jonathan Gregson pp. 23, 26, 82, 103

Dan Jones p.20

Richard Jung p.83

Mowie Kay pp. 120, 121

Erin Kunkel pp. 27, 75, 119

Lisa Linder p.37

William Lingwood pp. 24, 114

David Munns p.98

Steve Painter pp. 1–4, 6br, 9, 31, 41–44, 48–52, 56, 59–68, 71, 72, 77, 79, 93, 100–101, 112, 115, 116, 122, 123, 128

William Reavell pp. 5, 18–19, 21, 29, 38, 70

Nassima Rothacker p.88

Kate Whitaker pp. 10, 16, 106, 109, 118, 124

Isobel Wield pp. 11, 36, 90, 91, 96, 97, 104, 108, 111

Clare Winfield pp. 14–15, 28, 80, 107

RECIPES

Carol Hilker
Apple Cheddar Pie
Diner-style Cherry Pie

Dunja Gulin
Individual Pear Strudels
Peach Crumble

Hannah Miles
Apricot and Vanilla Tart
Blueberry Pie
Classic Apple Pie
Classic Tarte Tatin
Layered Plum Crunch Dessert
Nectarine Crumble Tart
Pear and Cranberry Pie
Pile High Peach Pie
Plum and Amaretto Crumble
Plum Crumble Cheesecake
Rustic Plum Tart

Janet Sawyer
Vanilla and Apple Strudel

Jenna Zoe
Bread and Butter Pudding with Grilled Peaches

Jordan Bourke
Pear, Apple and Pecan Crumble
Rhubarb Crumble

Kiki Bee
Banana and Irish Cream Crumbles

Laura Washburn
Pear and Fig Clafoutis with Almonds
Pear Slump

Leah Vanderveldt
Strawberry Crumble Cups

Lizzie Kamenetzky
Germknödel

Maxine Clark
Apricot and Almond Slump
Blueberry and Lemon Cobbler
Buttered Apricot Betty
Buttered Cider Apple Pie
Caramel Apple Crisp
Double Cranberry and Orange Pie
Individual Apple and Sultana Pies
Lattice-topped Morello Cherry Pie
Mango and Coconut Macaroon Crisp
Pineapple and Rum Betty with Coconut

Julian Day
Apricot and Orange Traybake
Pear Tart
Rhubarb and Mascarpone Tart

Rosa Rigby
Cherry Frangipane Traybake

Ross Dobson
Cherry and Ricotta Strudel

Sarah Randall
Berry and Hazelnut Crumble Cake

Suzy Pelta
Boozy Berry Mug Cake
Soda Pop Dump Cake

Tori Haschka
Apricot Frangipane Puddings
Raspberry Croissant Puddings

Will Torrent
Chocolate, Pear and Winter Spice Crumble
Spiced Apple and Croissant Bake

Valerie Aikman-Smith
Jam Jar Crumbles with Amaretto Cherries
Rioja, Allspice Pear and Blackberry Galette
Roulade with Provençal Peaches

Victoria Glass
Apple and Blackberry Crumble
Apple Brown Betty
Cherry Clafoutis
Chocolate and Berry Crumble
Peach Cobbler
Queen of Puddings